how to have
extraordinary
relationships

how to have
extraordinary
relationships

(with absolutely everybody)

LUCY CAVENDISH

Hardie Grant

QUADRILLE

In memory of my sister,
Nicola Juliet Cavendish,
and also to my mother,
to whom I owe every
successful relationship
I've ever had.

Contents

Foreword

You've most likely picked up this book because you have some relationship issues you'd like to work through. Maybe you've been working on them for a while by now and have at least a preliminary understanding of where they come from, and why things tend go the way they do between yourself and others. Yet in spite of your good efforts to figure this all out and have things move in a happier direction, the gap between how your relationships actually are, and how you'd like them to be, may be frustratingly fixed, and all-too-slow to change in any meaningful way.

If this describes you, then take heart, as this luminous book promises to be a game-changer. For the wise and wonderful psychotherapist, Lucy Cavendish, understands that transforming our relationships for the better lies not in simply analyzing *why* we are the way we are, but rather in equipping us with the necessary skills and capacities that would allow us to deepen into richer, and infinitely more satisfying connections with others. Skills you may not have learned in your youth, but which you now have the opportunity to identify and integrate into how you show up with the people who matter.

Creating a happy, loving connection is not a one-time static event. Generating authentic relatedness requires skillful ways of responding to the normal wear and tear that happens in all relationships, as well as an understanding of how to feed a continual stream of nourishment and love that can help each connection to realize its higher potential. For in order to have a great relationship, one must learn how to be great at relating. To become a person who understands how to generate true connection on a continual basis, particularly in the aftermath of hurt feelings, a misunderstanding, a disagreement or a difficult-to-resolve conflict. We must know how to continually create a sense of togetherness and trust in ways that will allow our bonds to ripen and mature over time, not in spite of these difficulties, but because we've learned to use these experiences to deepen love, rather than destroy or damage it.

Love might be unconditional, but relationships are not. For relationships require trust, and the ability to repair trust when it's been broken. Which is not something most of us were taught how to do, or even saw modeled in the homes we grew up in. Yet without this capacity, we will tend to feel insecure in our relationships. Fearful that they may end, or become stagnant and oppressive if we make a mistake or say the wrong thing. Imagine instead knowing that the bonds between yourself and others were strong, solid and resilient, and fully capable of weathering any storm you might encounter along the way. That kind of confidence is available to you once you master the keys presented in this book.

Given that our lives are either limited or leveraged by the quality of our connections, the willingness to invest your time and energy into learning the ways of healthy, thriving love is golden, and will set you up for a lifetime of happiness. For once your relationships are sturdy and secure, you will have built a robust foundation to support you to live your happiest, healthiest and most fully-expressed life.

May it be so for you, and for those you love.

Katherine Woodward Thomas

New York Times **bestselling author of**
Calling In the One **and** *Conscious Uncoupling*

Introduction

'It takes courage to push yourself to places you have never been before ... And the day came when the risk it took to stay tight inside the bud was more painful than the risk it took to blossom.'

Anaïs Nin

This book is written for anyone who wants to lead a life in which they are happier, more joyous, more connected, and more contented. It sounds an appealing promise, but how do we go about this? How can we find and spread happiness? What I've come to realize is that we can do this when we attain a level of contentedness that emanates from within us on a daily basis – a level of ease that moves us forwards towards a fulfilling future, in which we're able to have extraordinary relationships with absolutely everybody.

Modern life can be chaotic and stressful, and as a result, we often don't give our relationships the attention they deserve. Given the busy pace, and with so much competing for our attention, it's no surprise that our relationships become neglected or we get stuck in certain dynamics which impede our happiness and growth. Many of us experience a breakdown in our relationships (in all areas of life, whether romantic, or those with our family, friends, and colleagues) and whilst we may want to nourish them, we don't seem to know how.

Solid relationships form the essence of our wellbeing. They're the foundation for us making better life choices, for being better able to deal with challenges, and ultimately, becoming the person we want to be. When we take the time and energy to invest in our relationships, there's a ripple effect that spreads out across friends, family, co-workers, and beyond. Imagine a more welcoming and equal society, a better understanding of others, kinder communities – a better living environment both for now and for generations to come. Your relationships create your world, so the skills and practices in this book are designed not only to change your life but the lives of those around you.

Our capacity to have amazing relationships knows no boundaries. As human beings we have an extraordinary power and that is to choose to invest in our relationships; to be considerate, to take responsibility for our actions, to go above and beyond on a daily basis, and in turn see how this changes our relationships with everyone. For some of us connection comes in a solely human form but, for many, this also emanates outwards towards pets and other animals, our homes, our surroundings and our universe.

To forge stronger and more sustaining relationships with others, you'll first need to focus on yourself. I'll be encouraging you to become aware of your needs, primarily – to be seen and heard, recognized, accepted, supported, and loved, and how to have these needs met. As individuals, we need to feel we mean something, to someone, somewhere. Money can't buy this feeling because good relationships – those that are nurturing and life affirming – cost nothing. Our relationships, the way we structure them and how we are within them, is entirely up to us. It should offer immense hope, and emotional and intellectual freedom, to know that you can alter your life by paying attention to your relationships.

However, amazing relationships don't just happen because we wake up one day and change how we approach life and the people in it, and, hey presto, our world suddenly becomes transformed. I can't promise ease because this approach is a whole new way of looking at life, of behaving and relating, and that takes dedication and practice. This is what makes the rewards so much greater. It's a challenge but potentially it can lead to a root and branch overhaul of your life – of how you feel about yourself, your partner, friends, family, colleagues and, ultimately, the universe. It's a radical way of being – going through the world with this shine around you, emanating kindness, warmth, availability, connection, health, and joy. Believe me, it's magnetic.

MY JOURNEY

As a counsellor, therapist, and coach, my practice has been inundated with clients desperate for support. They're looking for help in every aspect of their life with many feeling lost, anxious, depressed, and lonely. Despite seeking answers, they feel disconnected and struggle with communication. As a trained therapist in many modalities, what I have come to know is that there is a central theme – most people need guidance when it comes to negotiating relationships. However, that support can get very expensive if attending weekly therapy. With this in mind, this book details the most common issues that crop up in my practice and distils the most effective ways to address them. The strategies I have devised to help my clients thrive are laid out on the following pages for you to incorporate into your daily life. And I know the tips and techniques truly work because they have turned my own life around.

The journey to writing this book started many years ago when everything started to go wrong in my life. It wasn't that all had been plain sailing up until then – like everyone, I'd survived all sorts of ups and downs over the decades and those were partially why I became a therapist. That year, however, contained such a litany of disasters that I was mired in pain. Betrayal, divorce, the death of my sister and then of my step-mother, near bankruptcy and the loss of my family home – it was devastating. I was lost and afraid in the very bones of myself and I felt I would never be able to move on from a place of intense sorrow and loneliness.

In my lowest moments I needed to learn a whole set of skills that I hadn't previously embraced. I had to learn to be vulnerable. I had to learn to ask for support. From there I needed to learn how to actually accept the support I was being offered. What I discovered was that it was my relationships that pulled me through. It was the learning of how to create amazing relationships that sustained me and eventually helped me flourish.

I started to see my relationships in a different light and came to realize that expanding into and investing in them made my life feel so much better. I started walking through the world as someone who was having amazing relationships with everyone I encountered – from family and friends, to lovers, and even random strangers on the streets. I felt I was bathed in some amazing light that emanated wellness and goodness everywhere I went. Life began to change. And now I want this change to be possible for everyone.

ABOUT THIS BOOK

In this book I will guide you through the seven steps that will uplevel all your relationships:

1. **Active listening.** Truly hear what those around you are saying.

2. **Empathy.** Understand others and let them know how you appreciate them.

3. **Change the narrative.** Move away from the negative stories you tell yourself that hold you back.

4. **Healing yourself.** View your relationships through a new lens, untainted by past hurt.

5. **You are responsible for all your relationships.** Be accountable, whilst making time for yourself and for others.

6. **You have choices – make different choices.** Recognize that you have agency to make different choices that lead to better outcomes.

7. **Being rigorous about where you put your energies.** Focus your attention wisely and commit to a glorious, connected future.

Drawing on a variety of different research and thinking, each chapter offers approaches and solutions to the most common questions that emerge in my therapy room, showing you simple and effective ways to improve how you relate to others.

Each chapter builds on the previous one to take you closer to having extraordinary relationships. You will aslo find practical takeaways to incorporate into your life, starting *today*. The final chapter – how we create better relationships with our world, as well as with ourselves and others – is the culmination of this journey. It is where the practical meets with the spiritual.

There are case studies from my practice to help bring teachings to life (with names and any other identifiable details changed to protect anonymity) as well as quizzes – complete each quiz as you finish the chapter then revisit them at a later date to see if your results alter. Every technique detailed has the potential to change how you view yourself and those around you. You will find yourself moving away from being potentially isolated, confused, disappointed, and disconnected to a place where you have sustaining relationships that revive and support you. By following the seven steps, your relationships with everyone in your life will transform – especially with those you *choose* to have great relationships with. Also – and maybe most importantly – you will have a much better relationship with yourself. It's an exciting thought; imagine waking up every day knowing that life looks good. You'll be in harmony with yourself and others, and you'll have the ability to repair ruptured relationships.

By committing to the steps in this book, by going on this journey, by making the radical decision to pay attention to your relationships, you will have relationships the quality of which you may never have experienced before. And it all starts with you – you have the power to change how you live in the world and how others respond to you. It takes commitment. It takes compassion. It takes you knowing yourself potentially in a slightly different way. This is a future worth having.

Chapter 1

Active
listening

'Happiness is when what you think, what you say, and what you do are in harmony.'

Mahatma Gandhi

The first step in improving your relationships is to practice the art of active listening. Do you ever feel frustrated with your colleagues, friends, or family? Do you find it hard to forge authentic relationships with partners? Maybe you even get frustrated with your relationship with yourself? Sometimes we can't hear what we need to in order to foster better, more considerate, connected, and caring relationships. This is where active listening can be a game changer in creating a solid foundation for every relationship we have. It's the one thing, above all else, that has the power to change your relationships – *all* relationships – and the quality of them, almost instantaneously. I first discovered how active listening can affect relationships when I was studying to be a therapist many years ago and had training in Imago Relationship Therapy[1]. A cornerstone of this type of therapy is its active-listening technique as espoused by the founders of Imago, Dr Harville Henrix and Dr Helen LaKelly Hunt, from their work and teachings in the book *Getting the Love You Want* (you can find many YouTube videos that demonstrate active-listening techniques, including ones by Dr Hendrix and Dr LaKelly Hunt themselves). For me, it was like stepping into an arena that I knew existed – one where everyone can hear each other

---

[1] Created in the 1980s by Dr Harville Hendrix and Dr Helen LaKelly Hunt, Imago Relationship Therapy is a branch of couples' therapy that seeks to reposition difficulties within a relationship into opportunities for healing.

– but didn't truly know how to engage with. Active listening is something most of us are aware of but don't know how to use. We are not used to listening to people with open ears, really being attentive to what they are saying. Most of us are just waiting to say what *we* want to say. Yet active listening is one of the most essential tools in our kit when it comes to improving all relationships. This technique can take us from out-and-out warfare to calm rationality and empathy.

In this chapter you will learn how to:

1. Listen in an active manner to radically and rapidly improve your relationships.

2. Respond in a way that makes the other person feel truly heard.

3. Understand why this is important and how it changes relationships.

Active listening involves being quiet, staying tuned in to the other person, and committing to hearing them without reacting – this last element is crucial. This type of engaged listening means putting ourselves and our feelings to one side in order to give the other person time, space, and attention. Another key part of this technique is to actively reflect a person's words back to them. Accuracy of language is vital (rather than making a vague stab at what they said, or using the words you wished they had) because it's what makes people feel truly listened to. It's also important to pay attention to body language. Ask yourself, 'what is the other person doing with their body?' For example, are they leaning towards you? Are they leaning away from you? Are their arms crossed? Do they have an open body stance (are they sitting with a soft body and looking relaxed), or do they have a closed body stance (crossing their arms or looking stiff and wary)? Is their jaw clenched? What is their facial expression? We can learn a lot by tuning in to someone's body language. It gives us helpful information and we can choose how to react.

It's useful to model a relaxed, open, and friendly body stance yourself – smile, relax your jaw, lean toward the other person, uncross your arms, relax your facial muscles. Also, be aware of the other person's breathing. Are they breathing in short shallow breaths? Make sure you become very aware of your own breathing. If you slow your breathing down and breath long, slow, deep breaths, the person you are listening to will start to calm theirs down too. This is what our bodies do; we attune to each other's bodies almost unconsciously. We also mirror other people's body stances. Now you know this, you will notice it all the time. You'll both fiddle with your hair, clutch your hands, cock your head to one side, breathe in the same way. And you have the power to alter these actions. Make a change and notice how the person sitting opposite you changes their body stance and breathing in response. This is like having a superpower, and it's very helpful when using active listening as a tool.

We have all experienced situations where we can tell we're not being listened to properly, which can leave us feeling frustrated. The positive effects of being actively listened to have a significant impact on our interactions with others. The message it sends is, 'I like and respect you enough to give you the time and space to talk without interrupting you.' In our noisy world, where it can feel like we need to shout to be heard, being listened to without feeling rushed can make us feel prioritized. So often in conversations we're just waiting to interject with what we want to say, eager to give *our* opinion. Active listening turns this on its head in a matter of minutes. It means we're really trying to hear the other person before we wade in – it puts 'us' to one side. Imagine how safe and secure your conversation partner will feel when you show them you are prepared to really listen to them, and that what they say is important to you. Imagine how active listening could change your relationship with work colleagues or your boss. On a basic level, people are so unused to being listened to that the mere fact you are taking in what they are saying and reflecting it back so that they feel heard is a game changer. It works with everyone – from the person on the supermarket checkout to the angry person who thinks you've somehow deliberately upset them on purpose. Once we truly listen to someone and repeat it back – 'wow I hear you've had a busy day on the checkout,' or 'I hear you are angry, because you think I have... (whatever the accusation is)'. You can then reassure them that that wasn't in any way your intention. You will be amazed at how people change their reactions. The checkout person smiles as they feel someone actually cares about their day. The angry person calms down as you have acknowledged their anger. The more you practice this, the more you will notice how differently people react to you. It benefits every relationship across the board.

There's also a cyclical benefit to the practice of active listening. When you model this technique in your interactions with your partner, colleagues, friends or anyone else, they will likely enjoy the experience of what it feels like, and hopefully they will be encouraged to do the same for you.

Case study
TREY AND JANET

Trey and Janet, both in their early thirties, came to see me for couples' therapy. They were arguing the minute they walked through the door. They talked over one another and were openly disrespectful to each other. They seemingly had no capacity to hear each other at all, locked as they were in some kind of endless and damaging battle to make the other 'wrong' so that they could feel 'right'. And they were constantly telling the other person how the other one felt. It was a classic case of she said/he said, and they spent the first session with me slinging verbal mud at each other. (Many couples might well recognize this behaviour – blaming and shaming, and talking about their partner as if they were the enemy.)

As the weeks went on, Trey and Janet showed an inability to really hear each other. They were both so intent on airing their grievances that they had gone from being a loving couple to something far more resentful, hurtful, and toxic.

Once they'd got their hurt and pain out, I asked them to try something; to talk from their own position. Rather than using the word 'you' (e.g. 'You make me feel…'), they practiced using the word 'I'. This is very important because there's a major difference between saying, 'You make me feel so angry,' and, 'When I feel you aren't listening to me, I respond with anger.' Both of them looked at me as if I'd asked them to recite the complete works of Shakespeare. But I asked them to keep going, to try and regulate how they spoke to each other. It's a practice, I explained to them – the way we speak to each other, and the words we use, are important. When we speak to each other kindly and in a soft or moderate tone, whomever we are talking to will feel far more able to hear us, rather than immediately lurching into defensiveness as they feel they are under attack.

My next request was to employ the skill of active listening, in order to help them really try to hear each other. I asked them to sit opposite each other and to think of things they loved and appreciated about the other person. I then asked them to express this to each other: one person 'sends' and the other 'receives' by repeating back what they have heard the other one say.[2] In this way, Trey (sender) said to Janet (receiver), 'I really appreciate your energy and how much you take care of our family.' Janet repeated this back, 'You really appreciate my energy and how much I take care of our family.' After each statement, they'd swap sender and receiver roles. By the end of the session, having truly heard each other for the first time in a long while, they were both moved to tears. Read on to page 30 to try this yourself.

I asked Trey and Janet to practice this way of relating to each other until the next session. When they returned the following week, I could see the atmosphere had changed completely. They were even gently touching each other's arms whereas previously, they had been very physically distant from each other. Both of them said they had seen their relationship improve. 'He listens to me!,' Janet explained delightedly.

---

2 This is what is known as the Imago Dialogue, but it's also widely used in many other therapeutic practices.

WHY ACTIVE LISTENING HELPS

When we actively listen and reflect words back as accurately as we can, we are building up what is called 'attunement.' This is when two people truly understand each other, whether they agree or not. It's amazing how quickly people's moods soften and change when they feel heard, particularly if it's a novel experience for them. Many of us, for example, did not feel heard as children (can you remember saying something like 'I feel hungry' and your parents responding, 'But you've just had dinner!'). I don't want to blame parents, teachers, or anyone else for interactions like this – many of our caretakers didn't have the tools or knowledge that is spoken about more commonly today. What this means though is that it can feel revelatory when we discover we can be heard by our partner, colleagues, and friends. It calms all communication down as it helps us all to understand each other better. Feeling heard engenders connected and committed relationships.

In the case of Trey and Janet, one of his complaints was that Janet never matched his socks up when she put away laundry. When he told me this, Janet – somewhat understandably – rolled her eyes. 'Is that my job?,' she said to him, obviously frustrated. But when I asked Janet to really listen to Trey and reflect back what he was saying, their connection deepened and so did their conversation. What he ended up revealing to Janet was his hurt wasn't about the socks (Janet looked somewhat relieved at this!), but that as he had grown up as one of four brothers in a busy single-parent household, his mother never had time to match his socks. He was the youngest son and recalled witnessing his mother carefully matching his older siblings' socks but by the time she got to his, she was so exhausted she gave up. Whilst Trey recognized this as an adult, the child in him longed for his mother to match his socks, just as she had for his brothers. 'I just want to feel I'm loved,' he told Janet, 'not that I'm an afterthought.' Once Janet had really heard Trey, this revelation deeply moved her. Rather than feeling angry with him, she now felt deep compassion. 'Thank you for telling me this,' she said to him and both of them were in tears.

This is how active listening can change and enhance relationships. Letting someone know we have heard them, that they make sense to us (which is not the same as agreeing with what they have said), and then naming how they might be feeling, will shift every single relationship we are in engaged in.

It works because it allows us to show the other person that we are taking in what is being said and listening to them without butting in with our own agendas. If our friend is trying to tell us how they feel, *reflecting* their views back rather than *reacting* enhances that relationship. It lets them know you care enough to hear them, and that you have the capacity to be a safe container for them (by which I mean you're not going to fall apart when they discuss something difficult or awkward). Then, as needed, you can reverse positions – you can let them know how *you* feel while they listen.

HOW TO TRY IT

If you want to practice this is in your own life, it lends itself naturally to couples, so that's a great place to start. However, it can also be used with families, siblings, friends and work colleagues, if they are willing.

> **There are three stages:**
>
> **Reflecting back:** 'I hear you say that ...'
>
> **Validation:** 'It makes sense to me that ...'
>
> **Empathy:** 'I imagine this might make you feel ...'

For more examples, read *Getting the Love You Want* by Dr Harville Hendrix and Dr Helen LaKelly Hunt.

With this in mind, choose a sender and a receiver, then follow these steps:

1. Sender makes a statement (it's best to keep the messages you send short).

2. Receiver reflects back what was said, e.g. 'What I heard you say was ...'

3. Receiver checks if they 'got' what the sender was saying and then asks, 'Is there more?'

4. Sender keeps sending and receiver keeps reflecting back until the sender has finished.

5. Receiver then summarizes what they have heard and asks, 'Did I get it all?'

6. If the sender does not feel 'got' they will resend the missing parts. The receiver then repeats these parts back to them.

7. The receiver validates what they have heard: 'It makes sense to me that when I don't match your socks, you feel that I don't care about you.'

8. The receiver offers empathy: 'I imagine that makes you feel uncared for, ignored, and unappreciated,' then checks in with the sender that this is what they feel.

Then, swap roles so that the sender becomes the receiver, to allow both parties to feel heard.

WHAT CHANGES WHEN WE ACTIVELY LISTEN?

In our impatient world, we have a lot to say but taking the time to truly hear someone reaps huge benefits in every relationship. We go from talking about ourselves (the I-space) to walking over the bridge into the other person's world (the You-space). The result is that rather than just waiting to say our piece in the conversation (the I-space), we shift to listening to the other person (the You-space), which means our energy is oriented to and focussed on them. As we looked at on page 25, this is a seismic change for most of us. It allows us to feel supported and more relaxed in our conversations, with the knowledge that our conversation partner will not react in a negative, angry, or defensive pattern.

Active listening lessens reactivity. Most of us are very quick to become defensive. If we get any hint that the person we are talking to may be about to criticize or attack us (whether they are or not), we spring to defence, which usually involves some form of counter-attack. This means that conversations can very quickly go into blame-and-shame mode, rapidly becoming aggressively charged before anyone has had a chance to hear what the other person is saying. I liken it to putting on our armour as soon as we hear the words, 'we need to talk,' whether it's our partner, boss, or friend who asks. In this instance, some of us armour-up and hide while others get their imaginary mace out and whirl it around their head before a single word has been spoken. As active listening involves staying calm, tuning in, and putting our own feelings to one side, it lessens this aggressive and reactive tendency.

FORGING EMOTIONAL SAFETY THROUGH OUR COMMUNICATION

Something I often remind my clients of is what I call the 'space in-between'. This is referring to the space that exists between two people – if we sit opposite someone, or even next to someone, there is a space between us where our two bodies are in a physical relationship, yet are not touching. I refer to it as being the energy field, which is all about the unspoken. We pick up more about how someone is feeling from their non-verbal cues compared with their verbal ones, which means we are hotwired to make assumptions about them depending on how we translate their actions. For example, imagine walking into a work meeting and no one looks up – how might you translate that? Or you're out on a date with your partner and they don't make eye contact with you – how does that make you feel? However you respond, the point is that you *do* respond because you can feel that something isn't right. That's the energy field.

Because much of our communication is unspoken, it's really helpful to lessen everyone's reactivity by speaking and listening. If we don't do this, we can't truly know what is (or isn't) going on with the other person. When we feel listened to and given an attentive and present ear, the energy field feels safe. When we feel attuned to the person we're speaking with, there's a connection, even if that connection is tenuous. It can also help promote a willingness to be empathetic, or at least to try, because when one person gives you their full attention it feels good. However, if the person who is supposed to be listening is on their phone or not paying attention, there is no connection and therefore, no safety at all. A lack of safety creates anxiety and tension, and so we can respond to people either in a chaotic way ('You never listen') or in a cohesive way ('I really appreciate it when you listen to me'). Behind all conflict is anxiety, rooted in disconnection and danger – for Trey it was the fear of being unloved and unnoticed. The way to assuage fear is to have safety through structured dialogues that show one person is actively listening and attuned to the other.

This might feel uncomfortable at first if we're unused to speaking to each other in this way. However with practice, it starts to feel like a wonderful way to relate to other people.

GETTING STARTED

Timing. Have you ever walked through the front door after work and launched straight into a grievance with your partner? Or into a work meeting or a family gathering and just started airing your 'stuff'? We've all done it and it usually doesn't end in the most productive of conversations. So, it's important to always check in and see if someone is available to listen rather than going from zero to sixty regardless. If the other person is not in the right space they can respond with something like, 'I'm a little busy right now but I will be available ... ' This means the sender (the person who wishes to talk) can feel reassured that time will be made for them. It encourages adult communication whereby everyone is prepared to listen to each other and respond in an empathetic fashion, which lessens reactivity. It moves the sender from the 'you/my boss/ my family never listen(s) to me' to 'I will be heard.'

Validation. All feelings are valid and you don't have to agree with a person's perspective to try to imagine it from their point of view. Your friend might be telling you things you don't agree with, but reflecting it back to them means you are listening and giving them space to talk, even if you are fundamentally opposed to what they are saying. Use the phrase, 'It makes sense to me that ...' to help them feel heard.

Appreciation dialogues. Of course, not all dialogues have to be about things that are 'wrong' or complaints; we can have positive ones too. Start with asking someone if they have time to hear you and when they do, begin with 'I just want to tell you how much I love and appreciate you.' Tell your partner, friends, family, and colleagues what you think they are really good at and everything will feel far more positive afterwards. Do this on a daily basis and see how life changes. Once you have mastered this, it's possible to have more dialogues that may be more challenging, giving you the confidence to raise issues in a considered way, such as, 'I'd like to share with you how I feel when I experience you as ...'

Tone. Concentrate with care on the tone you use when you speak. As soon as someone utters the phrase, 'We need to talk,' it's likely the other person will get defensive as they assume an attack, criticism, or complaint is about to follow. If there is also a whiny or complaining tone to the request, the other person will immediately become reactive – that is, they will either become aggressively defensive, or they will run away and refuse to speak. Try speaking in a level, warm voice, and bear in mind how you like to be spoken to, i.e. with care and politeness. Once we know someone will give us time to speak, we can take a deep breath and stay calm even if we want to raise potentially difficult subjects.

Talk without criticism. Reframe your communication to start from the 'I' space. By this I mean instead of saying, 'You did this ...' or, 'You made me feel ...' or, 'If I were you ...' try saying it from a place of what you experience. Rather than 'When you do X, it makes me really angry,' try 'When I experience you as doing X, what it makes me feel is ... and the story I tell myself is ...' In practice, it might go like this: 'When I see that you haven't put the bins out when we agreed you would, it really upsets me because the story I tell myself is that you don't really care about me.' The person listening can repeat it back. Try it out and remember how empowering it can feel for someone to know they have been truly heard. And imagine how amazing it feels to truly 'get' someone – to understand they are not angry with you about the bins because they are irrational, neurotic, or a nag, but because underneath, it feels to them like a lack of care. It's a completely different way of seeing things.

Zero negativity. When I am with couples, I ask them if they can commit to not engaging in negative speak about each other. We fall very easily into negative speaking. Sometimes we are so used to being negative, we don't even hear what we are saying. I hear this across the board – from couples talking to each other, bosses talking to their workforce, and siblings having their usual rows – and it's why active listening is so important. We also need to listen to how we speak, the words we use, and how we talk to others and ourselves.

Attunement. This is when we can really tune in to how someone is feeling and it's enhanced by active listening. It's when we sit back and really listen to someone and then take in what they are saying. It's why we need to pay attention to the language we use. We don't have to agree with them, but it is important for us to understand that what they are telling us makes sense from where they are. When we say, 'I imagine this might make you feel ...' the other person really believes that you are trying to walk over the bridge and meet them where they are. It's also possible to be reassured that you will get your time to talk too, and that you will be heard and understood.

3 key points

1. Active listening improves every relationship.

2. It takes practice but once you have mastered it, active listening becomes second nature.

3. It's one of the most dynamic, quick-fire ways to really shift average relationships to the extraordinary – it resonates with *all* relationships and *all* people.

3 key tips

1. Never start a dialogue in which you really want to be heard without first saying, 'Are you available to hear me?'

2. Always respond with empathy, for example, 'I imagine that must have made you feel …'

3. Make sure you allow proper time and space so that the active listening and dialogue can be wide and expansive, and anything goes, as long as it is said from the place of 'I'.

3 key actions

1. Give yourself and others (you can choose whom) three 'appreciations' every day. These can come in the form of notes, texts, gestures, or spoken words, and be aware of how this changes your relationships.

2. Practice active listening in every dialogue you have, mirroring back what you have heard.

3. Let people know that you are doing things differently from now on and teach them active listening techniques. This will encourage a ripple effect as they pass on the skills to their friends, family, and co-workers.

Quiz
HOW ARE YOUR ACTIVE-LISTENING SKILLS?

1. When your partner says, 'We need to talk?,' how do you respond?

    a) You say 'great,' then walk out of the room and do something else.

    b) You immediately start panicking, wondering what they want to talk about.

    c) You say '*You* need to talk? Really? Do you?' and then start talking about yourself and about everything you think your partner has done wrong.

    d) You respond by nodding, saying, 'Yes, I'm here to listen to you,' and then suggest you both take five minutes, get comfortable, and then start.

2. Your boss tells you you're not responding correctly to the directions they gave you in your work review. How do you react?

    a) You burst into tears and run out of the room.

    b) You start doing an internal calculation about how much they'd have to pay you if they let you go.

c) You start protesting and become defensive, saying in an aggressive tone, 'I *have* taken onboard everything you've said.'

d) You take a deep breath, count to five, and then ask your boss if they would like to go over everything again so you can truly understand what they think you are not getting.

3. A family member asks you to meet them to 'clear a few things up,' what do you do?

a) Block them on your phone.

b) Start racking your brain, wondering what on earth you could have done wrong.

c) Say you will meet them and then make a long list of your grievances while planning how to get your point across first.

d) Say yes, you're happy to meet with them, and suggest a neutral space. You ask ahead of meeting up that you each give the other time to say what you both need. You explain that you feel it's important you are both heard because, that way, you are sure whatever needs clearing up will be resolved with grace, dignity, and deep understanding.

4. You and your partner are practicing active listening but you find that, in your view, your partner isn't really listening to you – when they reflect your words back to you, they change what you say to what you think *they* want you to say. What do you do?

a) Say nothing and muddle along – you want your partner to feel happy, right?

b) Have a hissy fit and say the whole thing is a disaster and a stupid thing to do anyway.

c) To make a point, start deliberately changing your partner's words when it's your turn to reflect back.

d) Find a way to gently tell your partner you really appreciate the care and attention they're taking at listening, but let them know you need to feel heard, and so agree to resend your words to ensure they understood them correctly.

5. You and your friend have had a falling out and you really want to make amends, but your friend seems incapable of hearing what you want to say. You start to realize this is a pattern in your relationship – what do you do?

a) You don't really know what to do because you are convinced it's all your fault anyway.

b) Start thinking there's no way of changing the situation and that your friendship is over, assuming you will just have to either apologize (which no doubt won't work) or cut and run and end the friendship.

c) Phone them up and shout, 'Now do you hear me??!!'

d) You arrange to meet up, then you let them know there's something you'd really like to talk about. You start by apologizing for not having brought this issue up beforehand – maybe you hadn't really noticed the pattern before, or you thought if you called them out on it, the friendship would end. You state that you care for them and you want the friendship to continue, but that you both need to try and hear each other more, and in a non-judgemental way. You then ask your friend if they might be willing to try this out.

Mostly As

You need to have a little think about your avoidance strategies. It's likely that you manage to get through life by running away from things that might hurt you or go wrong. Practice what it might be like to listen to people – they might actually be trying to tell you good things about yourself! Find someone you trust and do an appreciation dialogue to get the ball rolling. Keep on practicing and imagine yourself doing this with everyone until it feels more natural.

Mostly Bs

Do you spend your life lurching from one form or state of anxiety to another? It's probably hard to hold your centre, i.e. the inner part of you that *knows* not everything is your fault. You probably have a habit of cutting and running – when panicked and convinced someone is going to blame you for something, you cut off that relationship and pretend it didn't exist, or elicit hurt. You tend to quickly adopt defensive behaviour because you are convinced you *must* have done something wrong and everything is your fault. Now try telling yourself a different story. Ask yourself, 'Is it really true that I messed up at work?' Find a mantra that calms you, such as 'I am valid in this world and not everything is my fault' – this will help support you as you listen to whatever it is someone wants to talk about.

Mostly Cs

Whoah! Show down. You are quick and fiery and respond angrily, probably before anyone has even said anything. While they are preparing to communicate something to you, you've not just got your defensive armour on, but you're whirring your mace above your head. For you, attack is the best form of defence. But remember, anger is just an energy and, despite the bad press it gets, it doesn't have to be a negative energy – lots of positive change can happen from anger. But in order for you to have amazing relationships, you need to take a deep breath and let yourself know you are not under attack. Be open and generous with your energy so people can approach you. No man is an island, and I would suggest your defensive anger keeps people at arm's length. Try softening, maybe accepting the fact that not everyone will hurt you – some people actually want to love and support you.

Mostly Ds

Well done! You have obviously tried really hard to employ active listening skills, and you have grown some new skills and capacities in order to do this. You are willing to see your part in a pattern. You take responsibility and listen to other people, and express your feelings in a responsible way. Good job.

Chapter 2

Empathy

'Being empathic is seeing the world through the eyes of others, not seeing your world reflected in their eyes.'

Carl Rogers

Empathy is one of the most important qualities we need to cultivate in order to have extraordinary relationships. It means 'leaning in' to try to truly understand a person, and, in turn, feeling we can open ourselves up to others who are trying their best to understand us. In real-world terms, it's a quality that supports us in our quest to see things from someone else's point of view, as we bring ourselves to a place of careful listening. If we can extend empathy to our partner, siblings, co-workers, family, and friends, we are showing we have the capacity to walk over the bridge to try to experience their feelings in the best way we can. It allows us to attempt to 'feel' their feelings whilst not getting swamped ourselves. Empathy requires us to put ourselves and our emotions to one side, even if that is for a fleeting moment. It encourages us to slow down, to notice if others are struggling, whether that's with everyday issues or bigger life events, and to offer support where we can.

It's not all about having empathy for other people – it's also about trying to find empathy for ourselves. A lot of us have a whole set of inner voices that tell us many, many things. Our inner critic is the internal voice that tells us we are doing things wrong, that we're not good enough, that we're an imposter whom everyone knows is just winging it. These voices keep us reduced; they make us lose confidence. In addition, they may mean we often struggle to project empathy and kindness towards ourselves, while making it difficult to truly empathize with others. Hard as we may try, we might find it difficult to feel truly empathic unless we can 'attach' it to an experience we have already had ourselves. For example, if we have experienced the grief of losing a parent or loved one, we may be able to find it within ourselves to imagine how the other person may be feeling – we have an 'attached' memory of grief. We may be able to draw on some inner experience of loss or sadness, anxiety or depression. From this place of inner understanding, whereby we have an inkling of what another person might well be going through, we can find some empathy. Rather confusingly though – and no one said humans were simple – those of us who have an inner voice that speaks harshly to us, often do the reverse. We are so aware of our own pain and how excruciating it feels to doubt our every move and criticize ourselves constantly, that we can become *overly* empathic, which means we feel everyone else's pain rather than our own (there will be more on this later in the chapter).

The truth is that enhancing empathy enhances relationships. That said, we need to approach empathy with a sense of balance. What about those who experience *too much* empathy? This might be present in someone who has lost their sense of self – the central core of their character – so that they become overly empathic. This means that they have an overwhelming sympathetic energy that floods out of them towards pretty much anyone and everyone, but especially when they encounter another hurt or damaged person. It's a state of being both difficult to embody and challenging for others to be around.[1] It is not that being over-empathetic is 'bad'. It's almost a state that you cannot really choose. It's as if something inside of a person compels them to identify with and help others, but this can become tricky if a) the other person feels overwhelmed by the outpouring of empathy, and b) the empathetic person doesn't increase their capacity to feel empathy for themselves. All the energy flows outwards and none flows inwards. Empathy requires a balancing act – too little and we appear cold and aloof, too much and we overwhelm ourselves and others. The most desirable form of empathy is when a person has the capacity to feel for themselves and for others. They can extend inwards and offer love and support to themselves, and outwards, offering love and support to others. Both are in appropriate levels so they don't sink into a mire of desperation about themselves, neither do they become so involved with the pain of others that they lose all objectivity.

Carl Rogers, the psychotherapist and founder of person-centred therapy, was pivotal in promoting empathy as a vital therapeutic tool. In this tradition, I draw on it too in my practice. I encourage my clients to tap into empathy, showing them how it can enrich our everyday lives, by focussing on ways we can react that are kind and helpful. The concept is basically that if we can find empathy within ourselves for ourselves and others, we can walk through the world as someone who has greater understanding of the human condition. This leads us to become more open, kind, aware, and attuned, and less reactive to ourselves, other people, life, and universal events. This chapter explains how engendering empathy can be hugely beneficial to our relationships as well as our own wellbeing.

[1] For more on the subject of emotional freedom, see the works of Dr Judith Orloff. She also has an online empathy test.

In this chapter you will learn how to:

1. Find and enhance your empathy towards others.

2. Find and enhance your empathy towards yourself.

3. Be a safe container for others (whereby people feel they can talk to you without judgement), and also for yourself.

4. Understand that the practice of empathy changes our relationships with others, including how people react to us.

5. Be conscious of how much empathy you are presenting with – is it an appropriate amount?

Case study
CHARMAINE

Charmaine, a personal assistant in her mid-twenties, worked for a boss who was constantly on her case. Whatever Charmaine did, it wasn't good enough, and she told me she was often at the receiving end of her complaints. When she came to see me in my practice, she was burnt out, exhausted, and disillusioned.

Talking about her job, she told me proudly, 'I am responsible for everything.' This was the first time Charmaine had said anything positive about her role at all. She explained how she helped organize every aspect of her employer's life, from running her diary and booking her dog walker, to remembering her friends' and family members' birthdays and sending them gifts. Listening to Charmaine explain their dynamic, it appeared to me the two women seemed intimately entwined – in the sense that their emotional lives had become overly connected in some way. I suggested to Charmaine that perhaps it felt like *more* than a professional relationship in that the boundaires had been blurred, as often happens in close working relationships. Charmaine thought about this for a long time.

'It does,' she said simply.

I wondered what had gone wrong. At what point did this relationship pivot, and why might that be? I asked Charmaine to go off and think about when it changed and why. She agreed to consider this over the coming week so that we could discuss it further at our next session.

I wanted Charmaine to get curious. Most of us tend not to be all that curious about other people. In fact, we're often not even that curious about ourselves. But in order to have empathy for others, we need to make a radical enquiry as to what is actually going on beneath the surface. Charmaine's experience was that her boss could no longer tolerate her. For Charmaine, it was all about her and what she'd apparently done wrong. She was making automatic assumptions that it was all her fault, rather than considering that something deeper might be going on with her boss.

I wanted her to question her assumptions about the situation. There were so many other possible scenarios at play – for example, perhaps there was difficult stuff going on in her boss's life that she knew nothing about. Maybe her boss felt she'd handed over too much information about her life to Charmaine, and as such, she felt vulnerable that Charmaine had so much intimate knowledge about her. Maybe the only way she knew how to deal with this was to withdraw or find fault, or do something else to redress the balance. Perhaps her boss was ill or something was happening in her home life that was making her edgy. It's of key importance to ask ourselves the salient question of what are our assumptions about the situation versus all the other possibilities. We can ask ourselves 'Is it really true that …?' or 'Maybe it's more true that …?' For example, is it really true my boss hates me and thinks I am incompetent? Or is it possibly more true that my boss has stuff going on in their personal life that is leaking in to their working life? Is it true that I am incompetent? Or is it more true that I am actually really good at my job, I work really hard, and my boss actually does appreciate me even though they might find it difficult to express this at times?

All of those scenarios could be true, although it was proving difficult for Charmaine to entertain them when she was unable to extend empathy to herself.[2] I was keen to take her to 'No I haven't done anything wrong. I am good at my job' and 'My boss must have difficult stuff going on in her life for her to behave this way.' What I was encouraging Charmaine to do was to extend empathy to herself so that she could connect with her inner knowing that she WAS good at her job. Once she really knew and could embody this, she would no longer sink down into an inevitable place of anxiety – the place that was giving her false messages. The 'I am not good at my job' was a false story and if Charmaine could have empathy for herself, she would recognize this as being so. It's much healthier to act from a place of what's more true than it is to fall into old, tired, unhelpful stories about ourselves. The empathic part is being able to extend the love, care, and understanding towards yourself, then outwards towards others.

---

[2] This internal enquiry of 'what's more true' is a technique I learned in my training with the therapist Katherine Woodward Thomas, best-selling author of *Calling in the One* and *Conscious Uncoupling*.

ACCESSING OUR EMPATHIC SELVES

You've likely faced dynamics in your relationships, whether at work or in your personal life, where you're second-guessing a situation or another person's behaviour, particularly if you feel the dynamic has changed. Like Charmaine, it's so easy to go round in circles, racking your brain as to what it is you've supposedly done wrong. Is it true that you have upset the other person? It may be. But it's better to *know* that than to spend days, months, and years being hurt and upset about what you *assume* they are feeling towards you and why, rather than just asking them.

What I encourage clients in my practice to do is to begin harnessing empathy, by asking the person they're struggling with what's happening for them. This doesn't always feel easy – it takes a brave individual to enquire about another person's needs. It means putting aside our feelings of hurt, regret, anger, shame, fear, or whatever else, and deciding to be curious about the other person. It's not merely that you are showing up by being prepared to walk over the bridge into the their world, it is also about showing empathy towards yourself. In order to live a purposeful and happy life, you don't want to be carrying toxic emotions around with you. The kindest thing you can do for yourself is to address these hurtful and messy situations, even if what you hear might well be stuff you don't like.

Sometimes it may feel inappropriate to put your hand up in this way. For example, asking your boss, the MD of a huge company, how they are feeling in the middle of a board meeting might not seem the correct way to behave within the company's structure! But some of this work can be done internally. That is, if we feel we are being treated badly, we can do some thinking about it. We can become curious about our emotions. We can be brave. We can focus some of our attention on asking ourselves why might X or Y be the case – whatever we are assuming to be true. If we can extend love and empathy towards someone, even just within our own thoughts, as it changes how we feel. If we really get attentive, we might realize we have picked up signs that our boss, friend, or partner is under stress or experiencing their own worries.

Holding on to hurt, pain, and resentment towards another person causes us damage, while extending empathy is so helpful because it turns this on its head. It acts as an antidote to toxic and obsessive emotions, and frees us up to move forward and enjoy life. In order to do this, we need to understand how to access our empathic selves.

> **Key questions to ask yourself to enhance empathy:**
>
> **1.** What's my assumption of what is true about the situation?
>
> **2.** Is it true or is there a deeper truth that I need to be curious about?
>
> **3.** How might I know the difference?
>
> **4.** Can I step back, take a deep breath, and try to see the situation with clear eyes?
>
> **5.** Can I challenge my assumption and realize that the story I am telling myself is not necessarily what's truly going on?

HOW TO TRY IT

Empathy has a healing quality that causes us to want to move closer to people and form better bonds. It's where transformation in our relationships happens. Here are some ways to nurture and incorporate empathy for yourself and others into your everyday life.

Kindness. Walk through the world as if you are emanating warmth, love, kindness, and openness. Smile at people. Talk to strangers in kind ways. Tell teenagers you like their haircut, clothes, or music. Offer older people help with their shopping. If you can, give money to homeless people, buskers, or street performers. Compliment everyone you see. Notice the bus conductor, the person working at the train station or café – show all you meet your appreciation.

Openness. Move through the world as someone who knows – who absolutely knows – that, at heart, *everyone* deserves a little love, warmth, and kindness, and then see how people react.

When you embrace kindness and openness, what tends to happen is that the world will change and open up in front of you like a bud unfurling. People will smile back at you. Relationships will calm. Your inner system – the voices that tell you negative things – will quieten. Everyone who encounters you will feel contented, happy, even joyous in your presence. More than that, you will begin to see yourself in this light – you will begin to change how you feel on an internal as well as an external level.

WHAT CHANGES WHEN WE INVOKE EMPATHY?

Many changes come about when we connect with our empathy. Empathy creates a safe container, meaning someone can tell you how they truly feel and trust that you will still be there for them whatever those feelings are. Moreover, it creates a safe container for ourselves – imagine if, when you are hurt, angry, and upset, you have the skills to transform how you feel and react by finding empathy for yourself. It's a transformative practice to be able to name our feelings and needs because it bolsters our resilience – it allows us to attend to our own needs rather than ignoring them, or needing other people to attend to them. Further to this, it helps us create boundaries – we need to balance our 'giving out' of empathy with the internal empathy we show to ourselves.

When engaging our empathy, it's helpful to remember that no one is born horrible, angry, nasty, or selfish. Humans find adaptive strategies to counteract our inner feelings. For example, someone who was shy as a child may mask this as an adult by being overbearingly extrovert. Someone whose childhood was chaotic may now cope by being a perfectionist and ultra-controlling in order to stave off the fears of returning to that chaos. We often find ourselves reacting to people almost spontaneously and if our reaction is a negative one, it may be because we've been reminded of someone we don't like or of a quality *we* project. Rather than reacting negatively, when we practice extending empathy towards others, it transforms how we feel about them as well as their characteristics.

UNDERSTANDING ANOTHER PERSON'S PERSPECTIVE

This requires us to try our hardest to enter into another person's world, regardless of how they are feeling, and then letting them know we 'get' how they feel. One way to do this is to let people know you care about and appreciate them. This helps them know you are trying your best to understand them. And even if someone comes back with a lack of understanding or is still unpleasant, at least you know you have done your best. You'll have nothing to feel bad about or fear and you can stand tall, empowered by knowing you extended understanding to another person. We cannot make people accept our good wishes – that really is up to them.

When Charmaine came back a week later, she let me know she had made the brave decision to talk to her boss about the situation. In their discussion, her boss told her she didn't think Charmaine really had her back and it made her not want to share things with her. Charmaine was very upset – she couldn't believe her boss had said that – and she was about to hand in her notice.

I suggested Charmaine calmed down and maybe thought of trying a more empathic response to her boss. For example, if Charmaine had said to her boss, 'I can see you are really stressed right now and you don't think I've got your back,' (i.e. *naming* what her boss had expressed, as we looked at in chapter one) she could then have gone on to say something like, 'and I appreciate you letting me know this because now maybe we can come to a working agreement as to how we might manage this'.

Charmaine's jaw dropped. I went on to explain that I knew this wasn't easy, especially as she had been upset by someone's words and actions, but this is where choices lie – do we choose to show empathy? If so, we change the 'dance' we are doing (see opposite). Charmaine's boss would then have two choices with her response: to carry on complaining or actually sit down with Charmaine and work on their relationship.

I am pleased to say Charmaine did exactly this and the last thing I knew she was still in her job and she and her boss have a wonderful working relationship. There is a fundamental difference between enhancing empathy and *showing* empathy. The former is internal work – that is, we strive to feel it within ourselves – but the key is finding ways to actively show it.

SHOWING EMPATHY

In order to tap into our empathy, we need to change the 'dance' of our relationship with another person. People often get caught up in a dance, a dysfunctional pattern that goes on and on forever – it's the she said/he said dynamic. The only way to change a relationship is to do something different. In Charmaine's case, the different thing was to really listen to her boss, and show her she was truly trying to understand her. This led to decreased reactivity – instead of her boss becoming defensive, she felt momentarily disarmed and softened by the quality of Charmaine's attention.

When I support clients in my practice through similar struggles in their relationships, I often suggest they do something unexpected. In the example of Charmaine, this was her telling her boss, 'I think that you may assume I don't take my job seriously,' which was not something she expected to hear. Drawing further into her empathic self, Charmaine might have said, 'I imagine that makes you feel under-supported.'

What is key in accessing empathy is to understand other people's needs. The need to be cared for, the need to be respected and heard, and the need to have our boundaries respected are universal. Once we really understand what someone needs and why, we can draw on empathy. To do this we need to be aware of our own healthy needs, by which I mean those adult needs that come from a place of authenticity – who we really are as healthy, happy adults, and what we can refer to as our true self.

HEALTHY NEEDS VERSUS UNHEALTHY NEEDS (AND HOW TO RECOGNIZE THEM)

It's important to understand our needs in order to be understanding of others' reactions.

Healthy needs might include the need for honesty, for your boundaries to be respected, for understanding, communication, and connection, and for mutual respect, joy, fun, and ethically moral behaviour. You might have a need for acceptance, kindness, forgiveness, encouragement, trust, validation, and safety. These healthy needs come from a calm, rational place and feel valid – we can expect for people we love and care about, along with other people in our lives such as colleagues, to meet these needs, or at least try their very best to do so.

Unhealthy needs come from a wounded-child place; that is, the areas where we felt hurt and were emotionally injured as a child. They have a different quality to them – they feel urgent and possibly overwhelming. Your brain might feel foggy or fiery, or shut down, but you are aware you might well be acting and thinking in an irrational way, rather than calm and considered. If, for example, you are someone who needs a tremendous amount of reassurance in your relationships, it's probably because you fear emotional abandonment. Any painful abandonment experienced as a child can lead to future 'needy' behaviour, such as begging for attention or feeling nervous, panicked, or anxious. In day-to-day life, anything that smacks of abandonment will trigger a whole range of overwhelming emotions. And when we feel overwhelmed, we act out – this behaviour can become so frantic and desperate that it becomes off-putting to others. When people are in a child-triggered place it's as if a five-year-old is in charge. They will act in ways that may feel unkind, needy, cruel, mean, martyrish, selfish, intrusive, or just generally too much, when really they are in a state of fear that their needs won't be met. They fear they will left behind, ignored, humiliated … the list goes on.

It's common to encounter behaviour like this but what if we take a moment to reconsider our response to it? What if we stopped and tried to extend some kind thoughts towards people struggling in this way? Imagine a man in a car park who is screaming at you in anger because he believes you have taken his parking space. Maybe he's having a hard day. Maybe he got up this morning and his children were tricky. Maybe his boss spent the day shouting at him … who knows? But what you *do* know is that he is angry and he is shouting at you. You may react immediately by being upset and angry yourself – 'How dare he shout at me!' might well be your immediate response. But what if there was another way? What if you could take a breath, let your adult, competent self take charge, and bring calm to the situation? You could even say to him 'You seem really upset and having this parking space is obviously very important to you so please do take it. I'm in no hurry.' This sort of response will likely diffuse a situation like this.

We have the ability to choose how we respond to any scenario. If we are overly empathic, we'll likely focus on people-pleasing – that part of our self that wants to do 'good' or be liked, – which means we dim down our own needs. So, for example, we are not responding to the angry man because we want to please him or because we are frightened of him, but that we are consciously making a decision about how we respond.

Responding in a way that is empathic is probably the right choice in this situation. People are often disarmed by genuine kindness.

However we need to watch that we are not falling into people pleasing behaviour. People pleasing is such a common trait, particularly amongst, but not solely, women. It's born from generations of people who have grown up in a society that has conditioned us to shut up and put up. This means it's hard to shake off when it seems a societal norm. However, it also leads in to a stance of being overly empathic. Overly empathic people tend to really feel others' pain to the detriment of their own wellbeing, whereby other people's needs feel more important than their own. Many of us get succour from this because the story we are telling ourselves is that we are a 'good' person, yet we often feel short-changed when others don't meet *our* needs. When this is the case, we need to let others know how we are feeling, rather than endlessly prioritizing the demands of others. Your needs are valid and important – this is how you hold a strong centre so that you do not dim down your emotional needs to others. One way to do this is to practice the art of being more selfish, asking yourself, 'Who am I in this situation and what do I really need?', while possessing a sense of entitlement that these needs can be met. Bear in mind that no one can meet your needs if you can't express what they are. Practicing self-care – i.e. doing whatever it is you need in order to look after yourself, be it time alone, joining a choir, having a hot bath etc. – will help build your capacity to know what your own needs are and how to honour them. It might be as simple as realising you're feeling overwhelmed and giving yourself some downtime.

Just because someone else is angry and railing at you doesn't mean you have to respond in a similar fashion. By meeting someone's needs – the need to be heard, the need to be seen, the need to be understood and validated, even the need for a parking space – you are completely changing the energy between yourself and the other person. Whilst I am not condoning the angry man shouting, I am encouraging you to respond in a way that suits you. You are not put on the planet to meet his needs but you do need to meet your own so you have the power to choose how to respond – to ramp up the situation or to acknowledge his anger and frustration.

HARNESSING EMPATHY

'Energy flows where our attention goes,' as Dr Joe Dispenza says.[3] This is how our brains work – the more we practice empathy, the more our brain starts to react in this way as a matter of course. This means soon it will become second nature to show and experience empathy. Keep the points below in mind as you begin, or develop, flexing your empathic muscle.

Mindset. Empathy doesn't just emerge 'on tap'. We need to prepare ourselves for it and there are a number of ways we can aid its manifestation. Meditation can help[4], along with becoming more mindful of our emotions. If you are feeling angry with someone, or misunderstood, stop, breathe and take time to tap into how you're feeling (as well as how the other person may be feeling) and everything will calm down.

Balance. Some people are natural empaths – they 'feel' for everyone, and it's usually obvious when you meet one of these people. Often their over-sensitivity leads them to taking on everyone else's feelings ahead of their own, neglecting themselves in the process. If this resonates with you, take care not to give away all your love and attention to others at the expense of your own needs.

Boundaries. It's important to be empathic within boundaries. This is what makes us a 'safe container' for other people.

---

[3] To find out more about Dr Joe Dispenza, look for his work on YouTube, read his books, or join his programs (https://drjoedispenza.com/).
[4] Chopra, Mindvalley, and Headspace are all good meditation apps.

3 key points

1. It's impossible to have extraordinary relationships without empathy.

2. Empathy is not only about trying our hardest to 'get' someone else, it's also about directing empathy towards ourselves.

3. We can grow empathy. It's not fixed but infinite, and we all have the capacity for it.

3 key tips

1. Empathy is not passive. It takes effort, skill, and commitment, so you need to engage with building it in an intentional way.

2. Walk through the world as someone who is abundant in kindness, warmth, and understanding. Smile, offer compliments, and initiate small acts of kindness every day and notice how things change around you.

3. Trying to enter another person's world is not easy, especially when someone is being rude, hateful, and toxic towards you. Actively remind yourself that change does not come through reacting in the same way. Model good, kind behaviour and you will be subtly teaching others how to behave in this way too.

1. Practice having empathy. Listen to people – lean in and really try to hear them, then feel in your body the emotions they are having.

2. Use gestures to show you are being empathic – touch someone's arm or given them a hug. Our non-verbal actions are as important (if not more important) than our verbal ones.

3. Begin a gratitude journal – I know you've probably heard this before, but it really works. Wake up every day and take five minutes to write down three things you are grateful for. Even if you have a horrible cold, try to be grateful for all of the days when you don't have a cold. It's as simple as that.

Quiz
HOW EMPATHETIC ARE YOU?

1. Your mother phones you and spends the whole conversation moaning about your brother and how selfish he is for never coming to visit her. What do you do?

   a) Pretend you are listening but actually you spend the call murmuring and playing a quiz game on your phone.

   b) Collude with her, saying you totally agree and that you also think your brother is a terrible man (even though you actually don't), because you are quite enjoying the banter.

   c) Let your mother know that you can really hear how lonely she is and how much she'd like to see your brother more. You acknowledge how difficult it must be for her when he doesn't visit and offer to speak to your brother on her behalf to express how she is feeling.

   d) Burst into tears. You cannot bear how lonely she is and how selfish your brother is – it all feels too awful.

2. You see a stag beetle trying to cross the local supermarket car park and realise it's in danger of being run over. What do you do?

   a) Ignore it and hope someone else will deal with it.

b) Get interested in the beetle but after watching it for some time decide to squash it in order to put it out of its misery.

c) Pick it up and gently move it to the back of the car park where there's a grass verge.

d) Wave your arms around yelling 'Be careful of the beetle,' bursting into tears because you are so worried it will get squashed. You then accept help when another driver offers to move the beetle for you before you spend at least five minutes thanking them profusely.

3. You are having a difficult time in life – major things are going wrong and you are struggling. Then a really good friend calls and starts off her usual description of how tough her life is and how she is fed up with her husband. Do you …

a) Tell her you're here for her but then put her on speakerphone whilst you start making yourself something to eat.

b) Tell her you are sick of her banging on and on about the same things for years on end and you've just about had enough of her selfish attitude.

c) Tell her patiently that you are actually having a terrible time at the moment and although she is your friend and you love her, right now you are not available to give her the sort of support she needs, and suggest she rings someone else.

d) Listen for over an hour giving her as much support as you can and really feeling her pain – poor her, your heart bleeds for her. I mean what is your pain compared to hers?

4. Your partner comes home obviously very upset about something and you ask if they'd like to talk about it. They say no but then continue to look hurt and upset, and their mood pervades the atmosphere in a negative way. Do you …

a) Say, 'I'm here for you when you need me,' but then find the atmosphere so difficult that you actually leave the house and go for a walk in the hope that everything will be better by the time you get back.

b) Stay silent for a bit and busy yourself making a cup of tea, after which become so annoyed by your partner's perceived passive aggressive behaviour that you find yourself shouting, 'For goodness sake, what's the problem? If you won't tell me, how can I be expected to help you?'

c) Let your partner know that you are there for them any time they want to talk to you about what's up. You tell them you can see they are clearly upset and that you feel for them. You then get on with what you were doing but inform them that you are close by if they need you.

d) Get very upset. It upsets you that your partner is upset and you want to make them feel better. You are frustrated that they are not sharing their feelings with you – so much so that you badger them to communicate with you and they get angry.

5. You have a colleague you are close to and work well with. Recently, however, you have come to notice that something is going on with them; they are late for work, they don't concentrate, and they have put up a few psychological barriers which means you find it hard to talk to them. On top of this, you are having to shoulder more than your fair share of the work. What do you do?

a) Contemplate talking to them but feel awkward – what on earth could you say to them? In the end you decide it's best not to say or do anything.

b) Find yourself getting angry. In the end, you lose your temper, telling them to stop being so bloody selfish and pull themselves together.

c) Suggest you go out for a coffee and then tell them you've noticed they haven't been themselves for a while. You let them know you've always valued your friendship and ask if there's anything they'd like to share with you, reminding them that sharing worries can be cathartic – you know, you've been there.

d) Feel hurt and sad but also very put upon, somehow also feeling that it's your responsibility to sort it out. You must have done something wrong or else your colleague would not be behaving like this – you want to apologize to them and let them know how bad and guilty you feel.

RESULTS

Mostly As

You find it difficult to empathize with people but that's probably because you find it uncomfortable to show your feelings to others. It's not that you don't have feelings and emotions (you absolutely do), and while you're able to see how others might be feeling, you get overwhelmed at the idea of doing something about it. You find it much easier to walk away and hope the situation will remedy itself. You might also feel nervous that if you say anything it might exacerbate the situation. Let yourself gently acknowledge this and then gradually allow the feelings in. Try naming them to yourself – 'I feel ...' or 'I imagine she/he is feeling ...' Practice this and notice the changes that start happening when you let feelings in, in a small and safe way.

Mostly Bs

You have great spirit, are a quick thinker and fast reactor – you are a 'fast-twitch' person. You have the capacity to be empathetic but because you move so quickly through the world, it's really hard for you to stay in 'empathic mode' as you lose patience. You have an intellectual interest in empathy but you find it hard to truly 'feel' empathetic. It may well be difficult for you to explore your own feelings so it is, therefore, really important that you try to tune in to your own feelings on a daily basis. Take five minutes every day to ask yourself what you are feeling, then write it down. Part of this exercise is recognizing that while you go through life at pace, others move more slowly than you. I understand that this frustrates you, but a key basis of empathy is understanding that not everyone walks through the world in the same way that you do. When you get frustrated, you snap. This not only makes people around you potentially wary of you, but it also means your fast-twitch response often leaves you exhausted and confused as people back away from you. You may even feel highly misunderstood, which is why practising naming your feelings will help.

Mostly Cs

Good job. You are empathetic but also able to offer people help and support in a way they can accept. You are a safe container in that you can hold space for people in a safe way – and this means people trust you and find they can talk to you. You also do this for yourself. You know where to place the appropriate emotional boundaries so you aren't swamped by your feelings and emotions. This capacity to keep your boundaries is what makes people feel safe and secure in your presence. They know where they are with you – you are consistent, thoughtful, and emotionally intelligent.

Mostly Ds

You are highly empathic. In fact, you are so full of love and empathy, that sometimes you don't know where your boundaries are and you lose your emotional centre. You let all your emotions overwhelm you, and you feel overly involved in (and sometimes responsible for) some else's pain. It's important to remember that this is *their* pain and while it's wonderful to be so aware of it, it's not wonderful for you to feel so involved. You probably think of yourself as a highly sensitive person. Consider keeping your emotions in check and remember that everything is not your fault or your responsibility to fix. Just being present, listening, and tuning in to another person can do wonders in its simplicity.

Chapter 3

Changing
the narrative

'Cease looking for flowers! There blooms a garden in your own home. While you look for trinkets the treasure house awaits you in your own being.'

Rumi

Changing our narrative is one of the most important tools we have when it comes to creating and enhancing our capacity for extraordinary relationships. Narratives are the stories we tell ourselves about ourselves and others. They may range from, 'No one likes me,' or 'Why can't people see how lonely I am?' to 'Everyone else is happy apart from me.' Narratives are formed as survival strategies primarily to help and protect us – they are the stories (some affirming, others not) we have told ourselves to get us through life. In the past, some may have served a purpose and they may have stemmed from often-heard phrases you might have been told as a child, such as 'buck up' or 'show a happy face.' However many are now redundant and the phrases themselves and subsequent stories do not serve us well as adults. Most of us have negative narratives that creep out, even if we can identify many narratives as being positive. It's the negative ones we are concentrating on here as they are the ones that hold us back.

In trying to understand how narratives form, an analogy I like to use is if we asked siblings the stories of their childhood, they will each tell a different story. None of these stories are true or untrue. Each sibling will tell their story from their own experience, how they interpreted it, and what it meant to them. But it's important to recognize that these stories embedded deep within us have served a purpose, but now perhaps we need to find a way of changing the story so that we can move beyond it. You may be aware of stories you have told yourself that perpetuate in the background of your life. The problem is, when we stick with the same story, we see everything through the same lens, the one which we've always seen things through. This means we will tend to approach relationships in the same way we have always done and this, of course, leads to the same outcome (if we put the ingredients for a carrot cake in the oven, it doesn't come out as a chocolate cake!). So, it's vitally important that we are aware of the stories we are telling ourselves because it is these stories that keep us in the same place. Once we see them for what they are we can change them, so that our relationships can be mutable and fluid, rather than stuck.

We have the ability to choose how we tell a story. We can retell ourselves a different narrative – one that makes sense, lifts us out of our usual patterns and, fundamentally, also feels true to us. As Maya Angelou said, 'If you don't like something, change it. If you can't change it, change your attitude.' We can't change anyone else, we can only change our own feelings about things, situations, and people, and this, of course, starts with us. It starts with a sense of the future we are committed to having, one where we are happy, secure, seen, heard, loved, and, even more importantly, where we can offer this to others. The key to changing the narrative is how you receive your own story and the knowledge that you have the power to change it.

> **In this chapter you will learn how to:**
>
> **1.** Spot your narrative.
>
> **2.** Change your narrative.
>
> **3.** Turn it from a negative to a positive.
>
> **4.** Identify the positive future you are heading towards. This is the place where your future self-resides – the one in which you are not held back by your old narratives that do not help you.

Case study
SARAH

Sarah, who was in her forties, was highly successful in her career. She'd run her own accountancy firm for many years and yet somehow felt she wasn't as successful as she should be. She came to see me to help her on what *wasn't* happening in her life. 'I feel so disconnected from other people,' was her weekly refrain. She felt she was failing at work, failing to make a good, lasting relationship with a partner, and her biological clock was ringing loudly. She was desperate to start a family but couldn't see any way of doing this.

Over the next few months, she told me her story. She came from a family where both parents worked from when she was a very young age. 'My parents worked so hard to afford to give me good things in life,' she said. This was not in doubt. She didn't want for anything, yet, deep down within her soul, Sarah told me she felt a paucity of love and care.

'I don't understand,' she told me. 'I was given everything, yet I feel so empty.' This feeling of 'lack' resonated throughout her life and, unsurprisingly, extended to her relationships. She did have friends – in fact she had many good friends – but she was loathe to call on those closest to her as she felt like a 'burden.' She'd had long-term relationships with a variety of men whom she had felt close to, but for the last two years she had been single.

She came to me with this one question: 'Why isn't my life the way I want it to be?' This is a question we often ask ourselves – why are we not living the life we thought we would? Why aren't we happy, successful, connected, contented, in love, and with good relationships with our family, friends, children, colleagues, the universe and, most importantly, with ourselves? To all intents and purposes, Sarah should be a happy and secure person living a wonderful life. She'd had what most people would consider to be a privileged childhood. But she wasn't feeling this at all deep inside – why not? I suggested to her that maybe she was constantly telling herself a story that wasn't serving her and asked her to go away and think about this. The question I posed was, 'What is your inner narrative?'

Sarah was desperate to know that there was a possible future, however remote, in which life *was* the way she wanted it to be. The fact that she was asking this question meant she did have a sense of what she desired. Once we know that, we can incorporate it into an intention that can set us forwards to where we want to be.

HOW TO FIND YOUR INNER NARRATIVE

In order to bring change into our lives as well as our relationships, we need to locate our inner narrative. We then need to grapple with it, shaping it until it becomes a more positive, future-oriented story that involves growth, connection, and adjustment. The more we uncover old, unhelpful narratives, the more we let ourselves *feel* them and the less we fear. By connecting to and naming a story we've told our self, we can become very interested as we hear the words the narrative is saying. For example, 'Everyone else gets the good stuff and I don't,' 'No one chooses me, no one will ever love me,' or 'I am not good at anything, I am a failure.'

Let's say an individual has a fear of being abandoned, which perhaps stems from a painful abandonment that occurred in the past, the pain of which still lies in their body. This may lead them to have an underlying narrative of being abandoned, the inner story being, 'Everyone always leaves.' Once they really let themself feel this, other feelings may bubble up, alongside a clarity of thought – maybe people leave but they come back; maybe some people leave but others stay; maybe they possess the power to not abandon themselves.

Remember, our inner narrative may well have helped us in the past. It may have made us resilient and capable. It may have got us to work hard at school, to do well at sports, to rise to the top of our career, but if it is causing pain or making us feel like imposters, then this story is no longer needed. When this is the case, we need a different story, which means we can thank an old narrative, release it, and move on.

Here is an exercise I often ask my clients, including Sarah, to try in a bid to identify their inner narrative.

1. Think of the place you go to when things don't work out as you hoped. Maybe your friend lets you down, or the house you wanted to buy falls through, or your colleague upsets you. Maybe the person you've been dating for a while suddenly stops returning your calls, or a family member tells you things about yourself you really don't want to hear. Ask yourself where you go to within yourself when life isn't going to plan. It will likely be a familiar place, one where hurt and pain reside. Question yourself about how it feels and what mental state it puts you in. Be very clear about this because it's likely a place you know well. It's important to name these feelings correctly as language has meaning and the feeling – e.g. 'I feel hopeless/I feel friendless/nothing ever works out for me and that leaves me feeling defeated' – will not be a new story to yourself.

2. Once you have found this place (which some call the 'void,' 'black hole,' 'horrible place,' or the 'sinking sensation'), breathe in deeply to connect with your body and go on an internal journey to find the story that is underneath the pain and disappointment in this place. The goal is to find out what you are telling yourself about the hurtful experience you have experienced.

3. Connect with the story around this. It may not be immediately clear. There may be fleeting feelings, whispers, and clues, but really try to connect with your inner voice.

4. Be curious – exactly *how* does this feel? Some people describe this as a feeling of existential dread or fear. Others feel blind panic. Some feel they will fall so far into a pit of despair and sadness that they will never emerge. Others have a deep sense of loneliness. Immerse yourself in this emotion and then name these feelings.

5. Once you have identified the feelings, think about where the energy lies in your body. Put all your attention there and concentrate on what the story is – allow yourself to feel it fully. Once we let ourselves fully feel something, often we are surprised by the fact that it doesn't feel as terrible or as scary as we thought it would. We fear the unknown and so this story needs to become consciously known – in the same way we unconsciously know it because we so often revert to it in our everyday life – and then we find the fear dissipates.

WHY MOVING ON FROM OLD NARRATIVES IS SO IMPORTANT

In Sarah's case, she came back into the therapy room and revealed what she had discovered about herself. She told me she had gone on a major internal journey of self-discovery as she linked her behaviours in the present with the feelings she had as a child. These feelings lay deep inside her but would emerge every time she felt upset. Her inner narrative, she discovered, was that she had a long-held pain of being alone, of being that latch-key kid who felt unimportant to anyone. On a deeper level, the lack of family, of someone being there when she came home – which contrasted with her friends' families, who picked them up from school, who turned up to every event, who had dinner on the table each evening – was excruciatingly painful.

These feelings that she was alone and didn't really matter to anyone dominated her world and had detrimental effects on her relationships. If the story we tell our self about the people in our life is 'they don't care,' this might lead to you noticing that you don't care that much about yourself either. Every time Sarah tried to move on to abundant, rewarding, supportive relationships, she would sabotage the opportunity because she couldn't help but default to her old narrative. As a child with parents who weren't there for her in the way she needed them to be, she had developed an inner narrative that she couldn't really rely on anyone. The story she told herself was that if she needed something done or some support or care, the only person she could look to in order to provide it was, and continued to be, herself. We can only change our narrative and replace it with a more positive and resonant narrative if we look at the fractures from our childhoods (as much as we can bear to). We all have a window of tolerance of the pain we can bear and it's important to keep just on the right side of this so we are not thrown in to an abject pit of despair. Generally speaking, subsequent fractures tend to build on our original wounds, so whatever pain we experience from formative relationships and experiences get built on until they feel like they're at the centre of our being.

Consequently, Sarah's negative script meant she would always work alone, either as a sole trader or a boss who kept herself apart from her workforce. She also found it hard to be in a group of friends, preferring to be on the sidelines, but then feeling hurt and left out when she wasn't invited to events like a girls' weekend. Very often she'd find herself feeling sad and lonely but didn't really know how to vocalize her needs in a way that people could hear them and take in, which contributed further to her feeling alone.

Do we need to know where our story originated?

This is a question I am asked a lot by my clients, who want to know if they need to pinpoint a story to a particular experience, and my answer is: not necessarily. This is because the most important thing we can do is change the story, and we can do this even if we are unsure where it originated from. Anyone who has had psychotherapy or counselling might have an inkling where their story comes from, and it's usually one from childhood – although many people are resistant to this. The good news is we all have the power to change our narrative. We can tell ourselves a new and different story – one that catapults us forwards into a future whereby we are not damaging ourselves, our relationships, and those around us because we are stuck defaulting to the same modes of behaviour.

Our feelings lie within our body, but despite this we often believe we can *think* our way out of our feelings, patterns, and story, when in reality, we can't. We need to feel our way into this new way of relating. By way of example, let's say, in your quest for self-understanding, you discover an innate fear of loneliness. You ask yourself what this fear is about and where it generated. Perhaps it stemmed from being left alone a lot as a child, or maybe you were excluded by friends, or maybe someone you loved left you. Whatever its origin, beneath it is fear, hurt, and pain. It can be easy to concentrate on the story (especially when it feels so poignant, so painful, so *true*, and so set in stone as if it will never change), yet it's the *fear* of the story, rather than the story itself, that will keep you stuck. As pediatrician and psychoanalyst Donald Winnicott said, 'Fear of breakdown is the fear of a breakdown that has already been experienced.' That is to say, we fear it because we have already experienced it and we know it hurts. It's ever-present and when we cannot let go of a story, its effects can permeate every part of our life, from having a pervasive (but unfounded) feeling of dread that bad things are going to happen, to finding it hard to show certain emotions or vulnerability, or to ask for our needs to be met. It's why these old narratives can rear their heads in the here and now, sabotaging our relationships, and why changing the story is so vital.

HOW DO WE CHANGE THE STORY?

Ask yourself, what sort of story might you really like to embrace and encourage into your life? Concentrate on the aspects of your life where you are doing well – maybe you are a brilliant communicator, or you have a great relationship with your children. Perhaps you are a pillar of your community, or you have a job or hobby you love. These are the places within us where we feel a sense of ourselves that is positive, forward-looking, and effective – and it's these we want to focus on strengthening.

In Sarah's case, for example, how could she have looked at her story with a slightly different gaze? She could see how much her parents loved her. She could see how wanted she was by friends and family. She could reach out to colleagues or fellow workers in her field and become closer to them. She could arrange to do more social events. She could try dating differently, expecting things to go well rather than not to.

It might involve a bit of discomfort to show up differently in our world, holding a new, more positive story dear to us, but soon it will become the new normal.

HOW DOES CHANGING OUR NARRATIVE TRANSFORM HOW WE RELATE TO OTHERS?

Changing our story is transformative because it means we have the potential to see our relationships through a different lens. It can impact our relationships in so many ways including helping us to:

1. Create stronger boundaries with others as we won't be reacting to people from a place of lack, but rather one of strength.

2. Notice and change our people-pleasing behaviour as we begin to see we are likeable for who we are, and that we don't need to make ourselves appealing to absolutely everybody in order for our needs to be met (which doesn't work anyway!).

3. Present our own needs and wants in a way that other people actually listen and respond. This comes from an authentic place where we are confident in how we feel, meaning we don't sound whiny or complaining, but centred and resonant.

When we approach relationships from a new place, where the narrative feels positive and encouraging, we tend not to become stuck in the same patterns as in the past. Further to this, when we begin to become used to who we really are – loved, supported, seen, and heard; a person who chooses to believe good things about themselves – our imposter syndrome starts to fade as it's no longer needed.

THE RIPPLE EFFECT OF CHANGING THE NARRATIVE

A key element of changing our narrative is to begin responding to people (including our self) with kindness and empathy. Once we relate and react to others through a lens that is rooted in these qualities, it fosters greater understanding of others. For example, when someone hurts us or behaves irresponsibly, we can try to stretch ourselves to imagine the negative story they might well be telling themselves. This lens allows us to forge stronger relationships because having empathy at our core enables us to hold others in a more tender way, and to remember that many people are grappling with difficult or unprocessed feelings.

Have you ever wondered about how individuals emerge from adverse childhood experiences (ACEs) or a less than ideal start in life? Consider those who have had a difficult childhood, perhaps living in an unstable home or one where poverty or abuse was present, and yet they turn out to be happy, balanced adults. Other people can go through awful childhoods and end up in terrible places, facing anxiety, depression, or addiction as adults. The question everybody always asks is, why is this? A significant reason is that the people in the former example tell themselves a different story. They don't dwell on the pain or let it mean something terrible about themselves. Trauma comes in all different shapes and sizes but it doesn't necessarily have to be so dramatic to our outcomes, but rather it's changing the narrative that's important.

When we change the narrative from negative to positive, we are changing how we show up in relationships. Instead of defaulting to a 'poor me' script, for example, we may choose to tell ourselves that actually, we are pretty fortunate in life. We may be able to find qualities within ourselves that we like and admire. We can choose to invest in and grow these qualities until we start relating to other people in a different way. And once we do this, we are essentially changing the rhythm and the dance of our relationships. When we change the dance and show up in relationships differently, others have no choice but to change their reactions to us too.

So, we are playing forwards what we have learned – once we change our narrative we are, in our own subtle way, encouraging others to do that too. When we think of our families, we can view our parents with empathy and let them know how much we appreciated how hard they worked for us, even if we haven't had a great dynamic with them in the past. We can then encourage a new dynamic whereby we spend more quality time together, for example. We can decide to let our partner know how we feel rather than simmering with resentment because we think he or she has deliberately made us feel bad. We can be enquiring of our colleagues about what is working well and what isn't. We can grow the capacity to turn negatives into positives – to feel good things rather than negative things. Keep in mind that no one can really make us feel anything, it's we who have agency and so, it's we who are responsible for how we feel – and much of this is based on the narrative we are telling ourselves.

On some level, it can make us feel safe to tell ourselves the old story because it's a familiar one; but while it may offer safety, it'll keep us stuck, costing us love, intimacy, and extraordinary relationships. The new story might feel uncomfortable merely because it's new, so it might take time to believe it, deep down in our body. Try to fully embody the change and let yourself take infinitesimal yet determined movements towards an evolved future. Practice the art of detachment by observing your story as if it were playing out in a movie, then ask yourself what you might like to change about this movie.

PRACTICAL STEPS TO BEGIN CHANGING YOUR NARRATIVE

Changing the narrative works to strengthen relationships because first, it fundamentally shifts how we relate to ourselves. This means we can access the power to choose. We can make our own choices about the narrative we are telling ourselves. So, we can ask ourselves, 'Is it really true that my partner hasn't put the bins out because he is lazy, takes me for granted, and doesn't care about me?' Or is this an assumption we are making? Even if we've stacked up an entire mountain of evidence that our partner doesn't care about us, we have the power to choose to change this narrative. The story will evolve – maybe they do care deeply; maybe they just forgot, or were too busy, or are a tad on the lazy side; maybe they hate putting the bins out and are hoping that if they don't do it, we will. None of this is about a lack of care – it's about behaviour and behaviour can be changed. What we are doing here is questioning the narrative and asking ourselves, from whose angle are we seeing it? We are all too quick to assume there is a truth – e.g. maybe my partner really doesn't care about me, but it's important to check this assumption out. People ask me about the 'truth' but really it's about the lens we are looking at things through. If you come to the conclusion that you are surrounded by people who don't care about you then you would need to ask yourself why that is the case, how you have let yourself get into that situation, and take action from there.

Awareness. Once we start noticing our patterns of negative thinking and assumptions, we can start changing them. It's as if we have a torch we can shine on our own behaviour and thoughts. This torchlight may well also create shadows, but the point is once we recognize how we behave and the narrative we are telling ourselves, we can make different decisions. This means we can start showing up in our relationships in a different way.

Positivity. Tell yourself a more positive story – fill in the blanks with something amazing rather than negative. For example, if someone says, 'I saw your social media post,' and then doesn't say anything more about it, fill in the blank after that with '... and I thought it was really funny/insightful!' Be kind to yourself by reminding yourself what you are really good at.

Agency. What we choose to think is a *choice* and we can make different and better choices. The place the story lies is within ourselves. We have alighted upon a narrative – one that maybe made sense years ago and helped protect us or galvanize us – but it is appropriate now?

Practice. Like learning any new skill, we need to practice changing our narrative, especially if it's a story we've told ourselves many times. Practice talking to yourself every day in a voice that gives you confidence.

Reframe. Turn negatives into positives. Even if you have had a huge falling out with your family, remind yourself nothing stays the same, even the most difficult of situations can change and evolve over time. 'I will never talk to my family ever again' can become 'One day this will change, and we will all be OK.'

Lastly, remember the Roy T. Bennett quote: 'What other people think and say about you is none of your business.' Stop letting other people's assumed opinions of you control you.

3 key points

1. Remember the story starts with the self. It's the place we go to when we are hurt, upset, and disappointed. It resides in our body and can be felt as that feeling of dread in the pit of the stomach.

2. Ask yourself what the story is and what you are telling yourself about a situation. Then name the feelings and be curious about them. Consider the evidence for what is true and what may be more true.

3. Let go of old narratives that are no longer serving you. Remember that they keep you stuck in old patterns and get in the way of forming extraordinary relationships.

3 key tips

1. There is nothing to fear from change; it's normal that people and situations do not stay the same. The key is to be adaptable and know that you have the capacity to embrace all of the changes by telling yourself an empowered story rather than a powerless one.

2. Changing the narrative starts with turning negatives into positives. Go from 'I must have done something bad,' to 'I know I am a good person and I have done nothing wrong. If X thinks I have done something wrong that's a 'them' thing, not a 'me' thing.'

3. Be attentive and curious to your thoughts and feelings – if we monitor our thoughts and feelings, we have the capacity and power to change them. There is *always* more we can think and feel. It's like wringing out a sponge – squeeze a little more kindness, pleasure, and positivity from each day. This helps support the narrative that our world is a great place to be and that our relationships are functioning well.

3 key actions

1. Actively tell yourself your 'real' story every day. Really know it and let it course through you so that you anchor it in your body.

2. Embody the authentic you every day and notice how differently people react to you.

3. Create a mantra so that every day you tell yourself good things about yourself, that remind you of your innate capability.

Quiz
WHERE ARE YOU WITH YOUR INTERNAL NARRATIVE?

1. You have created a piece of work that has received a lot of attention. You're pleased with it but also feel a bit nervous about the responses, despite the fact they're all glowing with praise. Your mother rings and says, 'I've read your work,' and nothing more. How do you respond?

a) You say 'Great, I'm glad you saw it,' then change the subject.

b) Fill in the blank after her sentence with '… and I thought it was brilliant!'

c) Ask your mother what she thought of it, before prefacing it with, 'It's had a positive reaction from pretty much everybody.'

d) Fill in the blank with '… and I thought it was terrible.'

2. Your partner of many years has forgotten your anniversary. He also forgot last year and promised he'd remember this year and cook you your favourite meal but – as per usual – this hasn't happened. Do you … ?

a) Come home then sit silently, fuming, refusing to talk to him.

b) Feel a bit upset but then remind yourself of all the other loving things he does. You remember that he's not very good at remembering dates such as anniversaries or birthdays, but that doesn't mean he doesn't care.

c) Heave a big sigh then reluctantly reach for your bag and suggest you go out for a meal instead.

d) Feel terrible, let down, disappointed, and convinced he doesn't love you, which is obviously because actually no one loves you due to you being unlovable.

3. You have started a new job and are understandably feeling a bit nervous. What do you do?

a) Keep yourself to yourself. People can come to you if they want to get to know you.

b) Arrive, smile at everyone, engage people in conversation at appropriate times and make yourself appear as friendly as possible.

c) Make a few attempts to smile at people but then decide that you'll keep your head down and hope someone will invite you for a sandwich at lunchtime.

d) Go round the room introducing yourself to everyone then ask them what they'd all like for lunch so that you can go out and buy everyone their sandwiches – that way surely everyone will like you from the off.

4. Your friend has been training to be an actor for a long time. It's a childhood dream but securing parts have so far eluded them. However, they have finally been cast in a play. You go and see them but have severe reservations about their performance and also, about the actual play. You know your friend will ask you what you thought. What do you do?

a) Disappear before the curtain falls, texting your friend to say that you had to leave because you weren't feeling well but that you thought they were great.

b) Gently let them know that there were bits they were good at but other bits that might be better were they to make some changes.

c) Tell your friend that you thought it was a good first-time role but that the play wasn't as good as it could have been.

d) Effuse about how amazing they were, how brilliant the play was, and how they are obviously destined for great and wonderful things (then hope they don't read the reviews).

5. You have been on a couple of dates with a person you really like. It's been a while since you've felt this way, but you are hopeful. It seems to have promise and you've talked about going on a third date the following weekend. However it's now Thursday evening and you haven't heard anything despite the fact you have texted them a couple of times asking what the arrangements are. Do you … ?

a) Do nothing but stare at your phone every five minutes hoping you'll hear something.

b) Text your date asking if you're still meeting at the weekend – you explain you're a busy person so you'd like to know and that, if you don't hear back, you will assume it's not happening. Then you get on making other arrangements.

c) Assume it isn't happening but then get angry and text them saying how dare they be so rude and what kind of person behaves like this?

d) Text them, apologising profusely for texting them yet again – you are so very sorry for bothering them but maybe if they could just possibly let you know. Inside you are thinking they obviously don't want to see you and that you must have done something wrong.

RESULTS

Mostly As

What is the story you are telling yourself? Is it along the lines of 'I don't matter,' or 'I am invisible'? Your go-to tactic is to shut down and avoid letting people into your world. In this way you can stay safe. If no one truly sees you they can't really hurt you, right? But that doesn't mean to say you don't hurt. You are also probably uncomfortable with any form of confrontation so you tend to avoid that by disengaging, running away, or changing the subject. Try letting yourself know that having disagreements with people is fine. In fact, it's normal. You can survive them, you can cope, you can make yourself safe. Make small, empowered choices to let people see the real you a bit more – the one with feelings, opinions, and vulnerability – and see how your relationships change.

Mostly Bs

You have wrestled and grappled, and have probably done quite a bit of internal work to get to the place you are now. You have discovered that being yourself and making the choice to view events from a more empowered state has worked for you. Well done. You choose to turn positives into negatives. You are able to avoid going down the rabbit hole and instead, tell yourself a more positive story that also feels true. The more you have done this, the better life has felt. You have the capacity to see things in a more positive light than maybe you might have done in the past. You are committed to continue evolving your own narrative so that you can flourish in your relationships and in life.

Mostly Cs

You are trying so hard and are partially there. I imagine you are curious about your narrative and are in some sort of hide-and-seek game with it. Sometimes you are able to grapple with it and evolve it, then sometimes it gets the better of you and feels overwhelming, so you retract and go back to your old ways. Do not beat yourself up about this. Life is an ever-evolving story and the fact that you are even prepared to look at it, be curious about it, and not run away and hide is a very positive thing. The next step is to peek behind the curtain for a bit longer and more forensically as time goes on. Remember to tell yourself where you are doing well in your life and use this as your touchstone for further development.

Mostly Ds

You have a strong central narrative that kicks in very quickly. It could be one of many but there's probably an element of an 'I'm not good enough,' or sometimes an 'I'm too much' narrative lurking around somewhere in your subconscious. Be very attentive to this and remind yourself that you don't need to make yourself likeable to everyone in order to counteract your people-pleasing tendencies. Let yourself fully feel your feelings – you will be amazed at how quickly those feelings will pass once you've really let yourself engage with them. Find a mantra that helps soothe and keep you safe, such as, 'I am more than good enough,' then say it to yourself every day. When you feel the need to apologize or people please, or you feel panicked that other people are judging you in a negative way, just stop for a moment. Don't do anything you feel compelled to do until you have told yourself your self-soothing mantra and notice how your feelings dissipate.

Chapter 4

Healing yourself

'Our sorrows and wounds are healed only when we touch them with compassion.'

Buddha

Healing ourselves is one of the most important things we can do to transform our relationships and comes at a key stage in our progress, building on the foundations covered so far in this book. Once we learn to listen to others, practice extending empathy outwards, and start to recognize that we are all dealing with our inner narratives, we move towards the realm of healing. When we actively practice listening and empathy, it brings us support both inwardly (as we listen to ourselves) as well as outwardly (as we listen to others). It allows us to engage with our emotions as we learn to accurately reflect how we are feeling – this is the work we are doing on our internal selves. From there, we learn the capacity to extend empathy towards others, alongside to ourselves. We then move towards extending our attention to our narrative as we endeavour to identify it and retell our inner story, so that it is more forward-looking and nourishing.

Beneath all this comes the glimmer of healing our inner hurt. When we react from a place of hurt in our relationships it's hard to find growth, because we get stuck in our old familiar patterns and so nothing changes. But when we look at genuinely changing our patterns, we endeavour to bring ourselves to a place of healing, and this is a crucial point in our arc of transformation.

Healing our hurt starts with setting the intention to do precisely this. It means making an active decision to no longer walk through life in hurt and pain, which causes us to dim down our potential to change. This life, in which we have extraordinary relationships with absolutely everybody, doesn't happen by chance. It happens because we commit to this work, this inner and outer work, that means we are making an active choice to live life differently. It means we take responsibility for what we do and how we are in the world.

This chapter focuses on three elements: self-compassion, learning the strength of vulnerability, and the power of self-acceptance. These are the essence of bringing change to our life. They are the transformative building blocks that take you from looking outwards to comparison and external validation, to focusing inwards with empathy and a sense of curiosity. As the founder of Taoism, Lao Tzu, said, 'Every journey starts with a single step.' I believe that healing yourself is certainly the most important step you can take.

In this chapter you will learn how to:

1. Show compassion to yourself.

2. Discover that vulnerability is a strength.

3. Find acceptance and peace within yourself.

Case study
PATRICIA

Patricia's life had been nothing but disastrous according to her version of herself. She was now in her early fifties and her life was one of lack. She was divorced and her children had moved out long ago. Her trust in life, herself, and everyone around her was at an all-time low and consequently she felt lonely, under-supported, and disconnected from everyone. She craved good friends but felt no one really understood her.

Every week she told me the same litany of woes and upsets; no one wanted her, no one would ever want her. She'd go to great lengths to tell me about how rejected she felt. It had got so bad that even her friends were sick of her moaning and colleagues had started to avoid her. 'I can see it when I ask if anyone would like to eat lunch with me,' she'd say. 'They run a mile!'

Over the weeks I began to feel very sad for Patricia, but as the tirade of negativity went on, I also started to feel slightly frustrated. Whatever I suggested, even if it was something low risk such as joining a community choir to feel part of something bigger than herself, Patricia would reject it. She couldn't sing, no one would want her there and, anyway, she didn't like driving at night. No one would drive her. This went on session after session – her woes, my suggestions, her rejection of my suggestions. Then the final plaintive cry of, 'Poor me. Why will no one help me?'

This struggle went on for many months and, over this period of time, it became clear that what was really going on with Patricia was that the key to her unhappiness was herself. Or more importantly, her relationship with herself. I suggested this to her one day, asking her to look at what part she played in this endless cycle of alienation and rejection. At first, she looked appalled. Then she was angry.

'Are you saying this is *my* fault?' she spat at me. 'Not entirely,' I said. 'But you are the common denominator.'

Here is the uncomfortable truth – no one can like or love you more than you love yourself. We may well want them to – we may well long for our significant others, family, friends, colleagues or a higher power, etc. to heal us – but unless we have at least a smidgeon of self-esteem, a commitment to change, and the capacity to take in the care and love others try to give us, nothing can change. Patricia's outright rejection of the fact that she could ever be loveable and her apparent inability to see this was about a deep-seated rejection *of* herself *by* herself meant that nothing would ever change for her. No matter what good things came along, she'd sabotage them because on some deep level, she didn't see herself as deserving of anything very much.

Many of us feel like Patricia – on some level we feel sand blasted on the inside. It feels almost impossible to change anything and every time we tiptoe near the essence of our pain it can feel so overwhelming that we run away from it. The idea that we are the source of the pain can feel overwhelming. Sometimes we go inwards and blame our self, telling our self that we must be a terrible person and that nothing will ever change. However, this simply is not true. Human beings have an amazing capacity for change and part of this starts with the commitment to heal ourselves. This sense of healing, of intention, of commitment leads to inner peace and acceptance of others.

I'm sure you've come across people like Patricia – stuck in a never-ending circle of despair, who suffer from low self-esteem and self-loathing. It doesn't really matter what anyone says to Patricia, she is convinced of her lowliness and unlikability. The problem is that her reality becomes a self-fulfilling prophecy. People get tired of hearing her because nothing ever changes, so friends give up, frustrated by her inability to accept any words of praise and kindness. In the end, Patricia effectively sabotages her own life.

Why might she (and many others) do this? On the face of it, it may seem almost impossible to understand why this might happen, but if we cross over the bridge and use our newly found empathy skills, we will come to understand that Patricia's self-sabotaging strategies keep her safe in her world. It may not appear that way – why would anyone want to live like this? But it's mainly because it's what she knows. For Patricia, the idea that things could be different, that she could be loveable, that life could be amazing, full, and successful was such an alien thought to her that it was terrifying. Her negative self-image has been a proven way of helping her get through the world. If she navigates life from the lowest common denominator and with low expectations, she will never have to deal with the pain of being disappointed.

WHY MIGHT WE FEEL CHANGE IS IMPOSSIBLE?

As we looked at in the previous chapter, when we view the world through a particular lens it keeps us safe. It might also keep us miserable, but at least we know how that feels, and with familiarity comes safety. What we don't know is how happy, joyous, and contented we can feel in a world where we like our self and people like us in return. It's important to ask our self why we feel that change is beyond us. Here are some common reasons:

1. We feel 'safe' within our own story, however painful that might be.

2. We feel nervous to let anyone in so we stay within our safety boundaries.

3. We have not created any evidence that life can be different.

4. We default to what we know so we set life up – usually unintentionally – to keep us exactly where we are rather than reimagining a potentially different future.

5. We don't know *how* to change or what it might look and feel like.

6. We're hard on ourselves, telling ourselves negative things (for example, 'No one likes me,' 'No one helps me,' or 'Life is terrible') that we then try to find evidence for.

On some level, we set life up in this way so that we don't ask very much of it or we stay in our negative mindset because the idea of change feels scary, difficult, and possibly painful. We may well surround ourselves with people who are also invested in us not changing – those that take from us or speak to us negatively, which keeps us in our loop of painful feelings about ourselves. It might be difficult to understand why people may want us to remain as we are, especially if this place is one of hurt and pain. It's important to recognize that not everyone wants us to walk through the world with confidence and high self-esteem, so gravitate towards people who truly care about you, people who want you to be the best version of yourself.

HOW MIGHT WE CHANGE THIS PATTERN?

First of all, I encouraged Patricia to start talking to herself in more positive ways. For every negative thought (such as 'Why does everyone hate me?'), I asked her to replace it with something more life-affirming (such as 'I am a likeable person and people want to spend time with me'). I asked her to try and do this as a practice – to wake up in the morning and write down three things she did well the day before, or liked about herself, or felt good about. I explained it as a generative and mindful practice, allowing her to focus her thoughts in the future. If we constantly tell ourselves everything is bad, then it will be. (The opposite it also true.) When we tell ourselves good things about us, we are strengthening the neural pathways in our brains to think positive thoughts and to perceive ourselves in a better light. It's akin to building up muscle memory.

The idea is that we can get out of our damaging internal communication loops and consequently see every area of our life improve. Nothing changes if we keep on doing the same thing. As we can see with Patricia, despite her professed desire to change, she refused to embrace that because it was too scary. However, once she started the practice of speaking to herself in kinder and more positive ways, she gradually started feeling better about herself. The change lies in action and that action is about the desire to embrace our healing.

STEPS TO EMBRACE HEALING

If we keep doing, saying, and thinking the same things, nothing will change, but we have the capacity to make different choices. Here are some practical steps to bring healing into our lives.

Embrace positivity. We can get very invested in our pain – it's much easier to identify with the sadness, anxiety, and fear we have had in our lives for so long, than to focus on the positives. It might feel almost impossible to change but this is about commitment. Speak to yourself in kind, uplifting ways, turning negatives into positives.

Self-compassion. Be prepared to be kind to yourself. This is key. We might have not been the person we wanted to be in the past or acted in ways we wanted to act for very good reasons. But we can now leave these habitual ways of being behind and embrace our change. First thing's first, it's important to let ourselves know we were doing the best we could with the tools we had, rather than beating ourselves up or sinking into blame or victimisation for past actions.

Gratitude. Write down three things you are grateful for every morning. There is *always* something even if you might not think there is. For example, if you are in physical pain, focus on a part of you that isn't: 'I am grateful that the tip of my little finger doesn't hurt.'

Awareness. Be mindful of where your thoughts go. It's a very helpful practice to be aware of our thoughts so that if they start veering into negativity, we can stop them and choose to invest in more positive thoughts.

Curiosity. Be aware of why you might be invested in *not* changing. Maybe it feels too new, too scary, too impossible. Be attentive to these feelings in yourself. Show them empathy and understanding. It might be that your way of being in the world was a habitual way of showing up that kept you safe.

Look to the future. Remember that growth is future-oriented. Embracing extraordinary relationships with people is about change, and change means growth and commitment to that change.

―――――――

Body scan

This is an exercise I often recommend to clients in my therapy room. We can access our capacity to change by doing a regular body scan, which is something I have learned through doing yoga nidra (a form of yoga that takes you through your entire body) as well as various meditative practices.[1] Pain and hurt lie within our bodies and so we need a somatic approach and then a somatic response (i.e. body-felt sensation) in order to shift this. The ritualistic breathing in this exercise calms our nervous system, helping us to start the day in a positive mindset. Because Western medicine has traditionally treated mind and body as separate entities we have, for a long time, resisted the idea that our mind and bodies are connected. Thankfully this

―――――――――――――――――――――――――――

[1] You can go to YouTube for many examples of yoga nidra, or look on the internet for local yoga nidra practitioners.

way of thinking has now moved on and we generally see ourselves as holistic beings with mind, body, and spirit connected as a whole. Ancient medicines, such as Chinese medical practices which uses herbs, acupuncture, and movements such as tai chi, have known this for centuries. This is now all wrapped-up in Western culture under the huge and aptly-named blanket of self care. Furthermore, this self-care action allows us to engage with our body, asking it what it is feeling and then attending to its needs.

1. As soon as you wake up, take a deep breath in through the nose and sink into your body, sending the breath all the way through it, starting from the top of your head and running down through your body, spreading everywhere including fingers and toes.

2. Notice where you have any pain and then put all your focus – mental focus and your deep inner knowing and feelings – on that part of your body. Ask your body what it needs – it may give you a range of answers!

3. Breathe in to this and focus on what your body needs. Pledge to pay attention to this area and try to put your needs at the centre of your life. Maybe it's more rest time or, conversely, more active time. Maybe your eyes are hurting (get an eye test!) or your stomach is grumbling (are you hungry?). Is your gut in need of support (perhaps you need to take probiotics)?

4. Recognize we need to listen to our needs and then endeavour to do something about them. This is where self care lies. It is very important as it helps us stay mentally and physically attentive and well. It also means, on an energetic level, that we are letting ourselves know we are important to ourselves rather than way down the list of what and who is important to us.

———

Blanket work

Here is an exercise that was taught to me by my mentor Andrew Wallas[2], the Modern Day Wizard, which uses blankets to monitor and shift our feelings.

1. Take two blankets of two different colours and fold them into squares large enough for you to stand on. Put them on the floor with a gap in between them, large enough for you to stand in. The first blanket represents the energy of where you are now in your life. The second blanket represents your potential future where life is wonderful and abundant, and everything is possible.

2. Standing in front of one of the blanket squares, take a deep breath in and start to focus your thoughts and feelings. When you are ready, take another deep breath in and step onto the first blanket. Close your eyes or

---

[2] Andrew is also the creator of Business Alchemy (https://andrewwallas.org/business-alchemy/).

lower your gaze. This blanket is the energy of now. Wherever you are hurt or stuck, let those feelings sweep over you and into you. All your pain, hurt, resentment, anxiety, panic, worry, sense of futility, and failure lies here. However horrible this is, let yourself fully feel it. Then become attentive. What is happening to your body? Have you slumped forwards? Has your breath shortened? Has your mouth turned downwards? Are you frowning? Really feel into your body and be aware of the physical sensation of this pain and hurt. You might want to cry, shout, or scream. You might even shake. But let yourself know this is okay. Breathe. Let yourself know you do not have to stay on this blanket for any more time than you wish to.

3. When you feel you have fully experienced these feelings, open your eyes and step back into the space between the blankets. Take deep long breaths. Let your feelings go. Let yourself know you are safe and well. Shake it out of your body if that feels important. Really release these negative feelings and thoughts. Be active and intentional about this.

4. Once you feel calm and settled, take another deep breath and step onto the second blanket. This is the energy of ultimate abundance. This is where your intention lies. This is where success, happiness, fulfilment, joy, fun, pleasure, peace, and desire lie. Your dreams are realized.

5. Let these feelings fully inhabit your body. Feel them flood in – all this happiness and joy where you love and are loved, where life is working so well for you, and you have great relationships with everyone. The universe is your friend and supporter. Really breathe this in. Let the feeling go all the way through you from the top of your head to the tip of your toes. Then become aware of your body. What is it doing? How are you standing? Have your shoulders dropped down? Are you standing a little straighter, a little taller? Is your jaw relaxed? Are you smiling? How is your breath? How is your body feeling? Take it all in.

6. Once you are full of this sensation, open your eyes, take another deep breath, and step off the blanket. How do you feel? Really notice the difference in these two states.

If you find this exercise helpful, do it on a daily basis. The idea is that you are shifting states from someone with a negative view of yourself to someone with a positive view of yourself. As we hold feelings in our body, this shifting of states from negative to positive helps engender profound change. Once we start feeling positive sensations in our body, the positivity begins to run through us and we start to self-heal. Once we begin the process of self-healing we can realize how we can take responsibility for this rather than asking other people to heal us.

IT'S NO ONE ELSE'S JOB TO HEAL US

However much we may want another person to heal us and however much they may want to do so, we are responsible for healing ourselves. Despite humans being herd creatures who need connection and are designed to live in groups or pairs, it's only as individuals that we can address our past, in order to have extraordinary relationships. We break in connection due to childhood woundings. We are born as part of our mother – a 'nursing pair' according to Donald Winnicott (see page 87) – but inevitably the child has to separate from the mother. From then on childhood can be a rocky ride and however hard our parents try, there are inevitable ruptures of connection along the way. The stories we make about these ruptures – where we believe we are not seen, heard, accepted etc. – are the narratives we need to rewrite as adults with our new grown-up emotional capacities. We often wish to heal in relationships whereby we feel as safe as we felt as a newborn baby, and this makes sense – we rupture in connection, we heal in connection. However it is not another person's job to heal us. They can provide balm in the form of a safe space, love, attention, and care, but the essence of healing is our work alone.

If, like Patricia, we project such a negative view on life, no one will truly be able to help us (and it will exhaust them trying). In a way, we are setting people up to abandon us, retriggering our hurts. However, once we start the attentive process of healing, of recognizing our pain and wounds, and making the commitment to heal, we can experience many 'ah-ha' moments. These are the times when something is revealed to us and we think, 'Yes, that's it! Now I understand,' or 'Wow, that's what I do,' or any version of these thoughts and feelings.

When we understand that *everyone* is pretty much doing the best that they can, given their childhood wounds and pain, we can access greater empathy for them. Otherwise, we set others up to continually play out our childhood wounded story. But this does not have to be the case and once we start healing our own wounds, it fundamentally shifts how we relate to others to a more positive and life-affirming way.

HOW HEALING OUR WOUNDS CHANGES OUR RELATIONSHIPS

Changing the script. We become less attached to our story so that we start shifting how we view ourselves. For example, rather than feeling that no one wants us and we are unlovable, we can identify that this feeling stems from a past pain that we can now let go of. Embracing a positive story about ourselves that boosts our self-esteem is not about faking it. Everybody has down days or time when they feel sad and anxious, but we can consciously make the choice not to dwell in this. We can walk through the world as someone who already has a great relationship with ourselves, who generates love, warmth, and contentment.

Empathy. If we are more understanding of our own wounds and pain, we can be more understanding of other people's wounds and pain.

Trust. If we can be more open and vulnerable to others, we can see this as a strength because we're not frightened of showing other people our underbelly. It's certainly not the case that most people are intent on harm; they aren't. If we let people into our lives, we start building warm, loving, authentic connections with others. If we build a protective wall around us, it keeps us emotionally bricked up, stuck behind our castle walls with no chance of anyone even getting a peek inside. We want to remove the bricks gently one by one.

Awareness. We become aware of our attachment to our hurt – both what it brings us and what it costs us. Once we know this, we can start relating to others in new ways that generate good relationships as we move forwards with healthy curiosity about ourselves, life, and others.

Consideration. It encourages us to treat other people with respect – we realize that they too are hurt and may or may not be in a process of healing. We can become more open and understanding. We build the capacity to 'shift centre,' that is, we can choose to be in pain and hurt, meaning we hide away or lash out, or we can choose to show up in the world as a warm, open, understanding adult.

Forward-looking. We are centred in curiosity – this is not about blaming parents or people in our past but deciding to treat ourselves and others with respect.

Boundaries. We recognize the need to establish clear boundaries with others. Healing allows us to move from a fear of being lonely and from people-pleasing tendencies to having greater self-esteem and knowing when to say no.

3 key points

1. Start every morning with a body scan and notice how your body is feeling. If there is any pain or discomfort, be aware of where it's located and send all your energy there. Be curious as to what your body is telling you.

2. Change lies in action. By 'shifting centres,' we learn how to manage our feelings so we take charge and make active decisions to shift our mood from negativity to a more positive state. Do the blanket exercise on page 115 if it feels helpful to you because this helps us locate and embed these good feelings into our body.

3. Notice those around you who support you as you heal and change, and those who wish you to remain as you are – be rigorous about who you choose to spend time with.

3 key tips

1. Realign your inner voice from negative to positive – tell yourself good things about yourself rather than critical, damaging things. This is a key part of healing.

2. We need to embrace healing from the inside out – this means seeing vulnerability as a strength. If you wall yourself in because you are afraid of getting hurt or being judged, you won't be able to establish close and fruitful relationships. When we dare to let ourselves be vulnerable and express our feelings, people will open up to us in return.

3. It is our responsibility to heal ourselves and be committed to living in a potentially radically new way.

3 key actions

1. Commit to this change in mind, body, and soul.

2. Let others know what's going on for you, explaining to them that this is what healing looks like.

3. Get excited about this – imagine how life is going to be once you are taking these steps.

Quiz
HOW HEALED ARE YOU?

1. Your friend asks you to spend a weekend with their very tricky and argumentative family. You really don't want to go but you know your friend would really like you to be there as you are a good social mixer and can help to keep things calm. What do you do?

a) Say you'll go and then spend the next few days living in dread at what may happen.

b) You become so worried about going and so nervous about what might happen that you find yourself totally overwhelmed by your feelings. But as the weekend looms, you start getting angry. In fact, you get so angry that you pick up the phone and have a massive shouting fit at your friend, telling them a lot of what you believe to be home truths.

c) You thank your friend for the invite and ask for a few days grace in order to give yourself time to think about it. You then call them back a few days later and explain gently that while you understand they would like your presence, you actually don't feel comfortable being there in order to ease the situation.

d) You agree immediately. Hell, it's a weekend away and you love a bit of drama so bring it on!

2. You wake up one morning feeling low. Nothing seems to be going right for you. You hope this feeling will shift but it actually gets worse as the day goes on. What do you do?

a) Call a friend and talk about it despite not feeling great about doing so – you feel you're constantly moaning to them and worry they're getting bored of you.

b) Go back to bed. You tell yourself nothing is going to change so you might as well just give up.

c) Decide to do something active to try and shift your mood; you go for a walk, do some meditation, or go to the gym. You focus on how you might break your low mood and commit to changing it.

d) You go out and get drunk and/or high. That always works!

3. Your colleague is finding a project they are working on very difficult and they ask you for your help. You are pretty overwhelmed as it is and it's not really your area of expertise. What do you do?

a) Tell them that of course you'll help only to then spend all your waking moments regretting having agreed to do so. You then become anxious about how you will cope.

b) Decide you can't possibly do it, berating yourself for being so pathetic that you can't take on the work to help them, and decide that you are pretty useless at this and, actually, pretty much everything.

c) Let your colleague know you will have a think about it. You then sit down and consider all your options before coming to the conclusion that, at this point in time, you don't really feel you can make a positive enough contribution. You let your colleague know you've carefully considered all the possible ways of helping but that actually you are feeling rather overwhelmed yourself and don't think you'll be that helpful in all reality.

d) Say no, you can't help – it's totally beyond your paygrade but if they'd like to come round and chill with you that would be great.

4. Recently you have begun to realize that you want to change the way you are living. You start cutting out various foods from your diet and begin to think you'd like to embrace a more vegan lifestyle whereby you only eat plant-based foods and don't wear leather, etc. However, your family are committed carnivores. What do you do?

a) Start thinking about how you might bring the subject up without offending anyone but then get so upset at the thought of your family's disapproval that you never actually say anything.

b) Convince yourself going vegan will never work – your family will berate you, look down on you, and never invite you to anything ever again. Spending long periods of time with them will be impossible. The more you think about this, the angrier you get.

c) Spend some time thinking about how to raise this with your family and when. You want to let them know that you wish to make some decisions about your lifestyle and talk them through your rationale. You explain to them this is important to you and you'd very much like them to respect your decisions.

d) You get very worked up about wanting to tell your family and then, at a family event, you defiantly blurt out that you're vegan and that you'll cut yourself off from anyone who disagrees with your choice.

5. Your sister – with whom you have a complicated relationship – calls you up one day and announces, out of the blue, that your parents are splitting up. As she is telling you, you get the distinct impression that she is intimating that she is closer to your parents as they have told her and not you. What do you do?

a) You are so shocked you don't really say anything but, once off the phone, get upset with yourself for not speaking up and asking more questions about what went on. But it's always been this way so you ask yourself why on earth you expected it to be different.

b) You are utterly incoherent with fury when your sister tells you. You realize you are sick to death her behaving in this way and you can barely even think about what's going on with your parents. You are so angry.

c) You ask your sister if you can have a few moments to take in what she's saying. You let her know you will call her back in half an hour. You then sit and really let yourself feel your feelings – shock, hurt, pain, confusion. Once you done this and you feel calm, you call her back stating that actually you will call your parents yourself so that messages don't get mixed up. You thank her for letting you know, then you gently, but firmly, tell her that you will take it from here now.

d) You are in two minds about what to do with this information. On the one hand, you are oddly compelled to ask more, despite the fact you are incredibly upset with your sister. You cannot help yourself but get involved with the drama which is, you suspect, precisely what your sister wishes you to do. On the other hand, you want to slam the phone down and say you never want to hear from any of them again. In the end, the drama wins over and you stay on the phone for an hour.

RESULTS

Mostly As

Do you find yourself tending to do things for others when you don't want to? I suspect you often say yes to things you actually want to say no to, but find it very difficult to do that. You come across as being helpful and kind, putting everyone else's needs before your own so everyone asks you to do things you don't really want to do. Your general good nature and desire to please people is not always the best strategy though. You are often tired by other people's demands but you don't really know how to say no. Try practicing saying no occasionally and remember, 'No,' is a complete sentence in itself. Listen to your intuition, take notice of your waving flags, and come to understand that people care about you and love you for you – they're not going to bail out on you if you start honouring your own needs by putting them at the centre of your life.

Mostly Bs

You are akin to a ticking timebomb. You are awash with emotions, feeling things fully and greatly, and you get hot under the collar and have real passion. Justice is important to you and anything you feel is unjust makes you see red. That or you become so overwhelmed you collapse, become ill, and have to go to bed. Part of the problem is that you internalize your emotions. Rather than telling people how you feel, you keep it all in and push it all down until it erupts either in a surge of rage or it turns inwards and you collapse. Practice taking a few risks – risk taking a bit more time to really check in with your feelings. Risk asking people to hear you and consider your feelings in a way that is calm and you will endeavour to be calm to. Grow the capacity to not just latch onto your first reaction but find the skills to then think a bit differently to how you have done before.

Mostly Cs

Good job! You have probably worked very hard on trying to access your feelings and name them. Rather than reacting instantaneously you have learned that it is absolutely fine to take some time out to think about – and feel into – what someone is saying, asking, or proposing. Rather than jumping into some form of action or unhelpful feeling state, you react from a wise adult centre. Keep on going but remember, sometimes spontaneity can also be fun!

Mostly Ds

You are a complicated soul. Part of you is wonderfully optimistic. You're always up for a party and people love being around you. You are seemingly a fun person who doesn't take life too seriously. You thrive on drama and you manage to avoid getting totally enmeshed in it because you can avoid all the messy emotional stuff by having a drink, getting high, or cracking a joke. But underneath all this, you might really be struggling with your emotions. In fact, sometimes you feel so overwhelmed by emotions that it's easier to just do anything but feel them. However, all these emotions are part of life. It's important we experience them and then recognize them for what they are – everything will pass. Once we can regulate our emotions we can have more authentic relationships and find ourselves more able to 'feel' in a way that is helpful and productive.

Chapter 5

—

You are responsible for all your relationships

'No-one can make you feel inferior without your consent.'

Eleanor Roosevelt

It isn't always easy to accept that we are, ultimately, responsible for our relationships. It takes a leap, a deep breath, an internal dismantling of the self, to a certain degree, to truly accept that the only person who is truly responsible for our relationships is us. We may think we are not. We may think that someone is trying to 'make' us feel a certain way but, it's down to us as individuals to be responsible for making ourselves feel anything. The buck really does stop with us, though this isn't something most of us are really aware of.

The issue is, of course, that in all relationships there's more than one person and therefore it might feel somewhat unfair to think that we need to be responsible for them. What about the other person/people? What is their responsibility? This is a valid question. When we feel someone is manipulating our emotions, we may well find it a difficult choice to take responsibility. A hurt, wounded part of us might want to retreat and cower, lash out or leave. We'll want to make this someone else's fault and to blame them, whether that's a nightmare boss, a jealous partner, a competitive friend, or a passive aggressive sibling. It might well feel like a giant step to recognize our part in these relationships, but until we do, these relationships will get stuck in pain, hurt, or mundanity, rather than shift and change. We can only heal in relationships if we take responsibility for our own reactions, and once we learn how to do this, all of our relationships will become more fulfilling. As Mahatma Gandhi said, 'We can't change how other people treat us or what they say about us. All we can do is change how we react to it.'

In this chapter you will learn how to:

1. Uplevel all of your relationships to make every one better and more rewarding.

2. Take responsibility for your relationships by finding the ability to speak words of wisdom to yourself.

3. Let go of what other people think of you. Once you fully grasp this, you can take ultimate responsibility for your part in your relationships.

Case study
ZAHARA

Zahara came to my therapy room seething about her family, in particular, her sister. She was 28 years old and felt aggrieved towards her younger sister who, in Zahara's mind, passed all the care of their ageing parents over to her. 'Everything falls on my shoulders,' she said. She told me she felt this had always been the way. As the older of the two siblings – to parents who'd had them later on in life – she had always taken responsibility while, in her mind, her sister had been scooting through life unfettered by any sense of care or duty towards others.

'Sometimes I actually hate her,' she'd say of her sister. She'd then promptly feel guilty for having such feelings. She'd hang her head. 'I don't think my parents even notice,' she'd say. Around three months into our sessions, I felt it was time to gently suggest to Zahara that she ask herself a few more probing questions such as why she had stayed quiet for so long. What had prevented her from letting those around her know that she was feeling this way?

At first, she was upset but I explained that what I was suggesting was that perhaps she had a pattern of feeling over-responsible. It was clear to me by this point in our therapy that she did actually take responsibility for pretty much everything, even when she didn't really need to, and I wanted her to reflect on that. She was also suffering from her feelings of being unnoticed and unappreciated. What I was gently encouraging her to do was look at *why* she might be viewing her relationships in that way. She had told me it wasn't just her family that she felt treated her this way, but that she felt everyone on some level took advantage of her. But what I suggested to her was that maybe

You are responsible for all your relationships

not everyone did actually treat her badly. Maybe some people did treat her with respect but she had a tendency to see every relationship through the same lens. More than that, if she looked at it differently, she might see people treated her better than she thought they did. I encouraged her to consider that perhaps her sister had no idea how she felt – maybe she actually loved Zahara and would help out more if Zahara voiced her needs and chose to treat her needs as important.

'The nub is,' I said, 'people will only treat you as well as you treat yourself.' What I was pointing out to Zahara was that she needed to take some responsibility for what was happening in her relationships. The key point is that it's important that we take responsibility for our relationships, and that starts with the relationships we have with ourselves. It's pertinent to ask ourselves: 'why would anyone love me more than I love myself?'

How is it possible that we are responsible for what happens in our relationships – surely if people are treating us badly that's their fault not ours? In a bid to understand more about Zahara and her frustration with her sister, I wanted to explore her pattern of behaviour. It appeared to me that she had a pattern of over-extending care to others and then feeling under-appreciated. I suggested three things to Zahara, and the first was that she had a choice. She could choose to change her behaviour, which would mean beginning to put her own needs at the centre of her life. This would result in her not constantly feeling that she was lesser than everyone else and that her parents' and sister's needs came before her own. The second point I raised was about her recognizing her own responsibility for setting up the relationships in this way. Zahara's response was that this was all unbeknownst to her, but I will always question that with people. We all have glimmers of self-knowledge at times, even if we don't like what that knowledge is. It's just that we get stuck in the story we tell ourselves. Many people have a martyr story and they often hold onto that identity very possessively, even if it isn't serving them very well. But we can choose to see the glimmers if we are inquisitive, brave, and committed to change. My third suggestion was that she take a step back and see the relationships from a slightly different viewpoint. For example, did her sister truly not take responsibility for their parents or could it be that she wasn't aware that Zahara needed more help?

To do these three things, Zahara needed to shift her centre of being. By this I mean she needed to stop seeing herself as someone who had to do everything herself but as someone who could develop the capacity to voice her needs and concerns. Sometimes staying silent is not the best policy.

Many of us find we can be very harsh on ourselves, admonishing ourselves for letting people come into our lives that treat us badly. We can get very stuck in the trope of everyone being terrible and uncaring without addressing the crux of the issue. When we default to a role (such as martyr, protagonist, black sheep, helper, or non-complainer), it's key to recognize this and important to understand why, because until we take responsibility for our patterns in our relationships, we'll stay 'stuck' and nothing will change. Also, whatever we are telling ourselves about ourselves, it may well not be true. We often think things won't change yet inside we know that situations and feelings can change all the time. We don't have a crystal ball, but some of us act as if we do, so nothing changes from that place. It's our ability to change our thoughts and actions that can lead to better and more fulfilling relationships – this is where taking responsibility lies.

In Zahara's case, she was firmly fixated on her role as a martyr. In her eyes, the more she gave, the more people took. This meant that she could quite happily sit in the place of 'hard done by,' letting everyone else know that she was a Good Person whilst everyone else was 'bad.' When she first started seeing me, Zahara couldn't really conceive that she was at the centre of this dynamic. For her, everyone else was at fault but nothing was ever going to shift unless she stood back, saw her part in this dynamic, and then changed her actions and reactions, including letting her sister know she needed more help. She could inform her parents that while she loved them, she was now going to let their other daughter step in. Even more importantly, she could prioritize her own needs in her life.

An integral part of my support of Zahara was to help her see that she could choose to change the lens through which she saw her life. I wanted her to become curious about how this pattern had come about. The main reason people sit in positions that look uncomfortable to the rest of us is that it's not uncomfortable for them. From the outside world that might appear quite odd – why would someone actually want to be so put upon, unnoticed, unthanked, and unseen? The truth is, we become accustomed to these dynamics over time. It was comfortable to Zahara to complain because it was what she was used to doing. It didn't make her happy or contented though, and she had the capacity to recognize this and ask for help – taking responsibility for our relationships involves *action*. Read on to see how you might go about this.

HOW DO WE TAKE RESPONSIBILITY FOR OUR RELATIONSHIPS AND BRING ABOUT CHANGE?

Here are some practical steps to help you consider your relationships in a new light and take responsibility for them:

1. Instead of blaming other people for things, look inside and be rigorously honest about your role.

2. Name your responsibility, for example, 'It's my responsibility to be a good friend and this is what being a good friend could look like …'

3. Reframe your grievances, so instead of saying, 'My partner doesn't care about my needs,' try turning this into something more like, 'Do I actually let my partner know what my needs are?'

4. Ask yourself how you could let people into your world a little more, so that relationships can change and improve. No one knows our inner world more than we do.

5. The action of taking responsibility means becoming aware of your role in the dynamic and the feelings that emerge as a result, for example, 'If I had let my co-worker know I am too busy to take on another project, rather than feeling I had to say yes to show I am a good person, I wouldn't be so angry and tired now.'

6. Vow to do things differently going forwards and make a pledge to yourself that you will start being more honest with yourself and others.

7. Try shifting viewpoints to see if your perspective is actually true or whether it's coloured by your relationship to yourself and others. For example, ask yourself, 'Is it true that my boss doesn't like me?' It may well be an uneasy fit in terms of personalities, but is it actually true they don't like you or is it more likely that they are busy and stressed, or that you both have different ways of working? Try to name the other stories that could be present to yourself, so you can tell yourself a more helpful story that comes from a more informed perspective.

Taking responsibility means moving relationships forward

What helps us to move forwards is the realization that we need to have boundaries within our all of our relationships. When I talked to Zahara about boundaries she looked confused, as like many people, she wasn't familiar with the concept – either its meaning or its practice in her relationships. I had come to the conclusion from talking to Zahara over the months that boundaries were missing from her upbringing, and that this was affecting her relationships as an adult. For anyone who has grown up in a household where there really weren't any boundaries, whereby people came and went, said whatever they wanted to say, and acted in any way they liked, how would a child know what boundaries are? Clients often ask why boundaries are important, especially when it comes to the concept of taking responsibility. Boundaries are about knowing our worth and feeling we are strong enough in our self to tell people what is okay and what isn't okay. This means we need to be in an evolved adult space.

When we look at taking responsibility for our relationships, what we are really talking about is growing them, moving them from a child-child space to an adult-adult space. This means not acting from a hurt inner child perspective whereby we are triggered by anything, however small, as we translate people's actions or lack of actions as being about us rather than *them*. Instead we can stand back a bit and ask ourselves some more adult questions, and see things from a more grown-up perspective.

Part of this requires having a deep acceptance and knowledge that there is nothing we can do about anyone else's feelings and actions. We can't make people act in one way or another, but we can change how *we* feel about the situation and *we* can control what *we* do. We can recognize our part in our relationships and take responsibility for this. So, for example, Zahara could say to her sister, 'I apologize for not raising this issue about our parents' needs before. I've wanted to for a while but I didn't know how to do it. I was scared you'd get angry with me and reject me, and maybe you will *but* it's not okay for you to not help out with our parents, and I'd really like you to do more.'

If you were to take this one step further, Zahara could also make a guarantee to her sister that they would work together. Whereas previously Zahara might have been tempted to launch into a critique of her sister and her lack of involvement with their parents (likely causing her sister to go on the defensive), this time Zahara could take responsibility. She could shift her feeling of not being supported and taken for granted by naming her responsibilities towards the relationship and taking actions to change it. Perhaps they could make a list of duties needed and how to divide them up, or maybe they could meet up once a week to plan their parents' care.

A new approach like this isn't always easy – after all, we're attempting to change habits that have been formed over years. Taking responsibility is key in helping us change our patterns of behaviour, because it allows us to own up to our part in them. In order to do this, we need to have an honest look at our own relationships.

HOW TO EXPLORE YOUR RELATIONSHIPS

We are relational creatures, by this I mean we are born in relationships (with our birth mother) and we are hotwired to connect with other people. Very few of us are complete loners and live the life of a hermit, so we need to develop an understanding of our various relationships in order to find some healing. This will allow that nightmare boss who may loom large in your life to become reduced to a more appropriate size in your psyche. The jealous partner's feelings can become assuaged if we take some responsibility and communicate with them about their feelings (which come from fear) so that we can understand them better and then make decisions from that place (i.e. do we wish to stay in this relationship). The people-pleasing sibling can be released from their passive-aggressive viewpoint. Life from this perspective looks like an enticing place to live.

Here's an exercise that will help you to uncover your feelings about a particular relationship.

1. Think of someone with whom you have a 'charged' relationship – that is, one that feels uncomfortable, tricky, overly exciting, etc. (rather than one that is calm and considered).

2. How did you get to know this person? What drew you to them? If they are a member of your family or someone you've known all your life, just think about what the relationship is like between you.

3. Find some words to describe them and write them down. What are they like, for example. Are they aloof, exciting, brave, dismissive, abandoning, overly affectionate, demanding, etc.?

4. Think about your relationship with them. What do you like about it? What don't you like about it?

5. Write down who you think you are in this relationship. Are you fully yourself or are you different to the person you consider yourself to be?

6. Why might this be? Do they 'make' you feel a certain way? Craft a few sentences that encapsulates your relationship with them. Who and what are they to you? Who and what do you think you are to them?

7. Now re-read everything you have written. What part of you can take some responsibility for what happens or doesn't happen in this relationship? This won't be easy, but it is important. Maybe you ignored red flags or dumbed down your knowing? Perhaps you turn yourself inside out like a glove puppet to keep this person happy and onside? Maybe you push them away or are overly critical of them?

8. See if you can take even a little bit of responsibility as to how this relationship doesn't work in the way you'd like it to. Write down what that might be, starting with the words 'I take responsibility for ...'

9. Make amends with this person either within yourself or maybe even face-to-face. Then make amends with yourself. This is where understanding and forgiveness lie. Try to understand what the reason is for this relationship not being as you would like it to be. For example, you didn't let them into your world and so they don't really know how to fully 'be' with you. Then vow to change this, so you let this person in a bit more. You also let yourself know the reason why you didn't let them in – maybe you were scared of being hurt or abandoned. This is understandable and this is where the amends lie, but let yourself know you are committed to having a different relationship that is more honest and empowered from this moment forwards.

We are the source of our own experience and so we show up in relationships in ways that generate evidence of the wounded parts of ourselves. How our needs were met in childhood has a role to play in our adult relationships. For example, if we felt ignored as a child, as adults we will find it hard to let people know what our needs are and expect them to be responded to. If we were smothered with love as a child, we might find ourselves becoming an aloof adult with a reputation for being stand-offish. If we were praised for being academic rather than just being ourselves, we will strive to do well in everything, in order to be loved, rather than feeling loved for who we are. If we had a parent who was an addict and whose behaviour was erratic, we will possibly be hyper alert and overly sensitive to any form of inconsistent behaviour, and we might well stay emotionally alone out of fear rather than choice. We might think that it's only us who can keep ourselves safe. If there was a lot of conflict around us as a child, we may grow up to be conflict averse so we people please to avoid any perceived drama or 'threat,' but this means we may never speak up. We might meet everyone else's needs but not our own.

It's a very difficult feeling to know that we are the source of our relationships. However, once we start to look for patterns in our relationships and how we set them up, we will begin to accept responsibility for wherever we're centred being where we are running our life from. We need to take action from our wise adult self, not our unruly child self who is intent on blaming others as well as our self for the mess of our relationships. Then we can tap into the part of our self that has wisdom, power, and objectivity. Our younger self will want to make others responsible for us and our feelings, allowing us to possibly shirk our responsibilities and shrug off our feelings. But this will not help engender extraordinary relationships.

HOW DOES TAKING RESPONSIBILITY HELP US TO CREATE EXTRAORDINARY RELATIONSHIPS?

In every relationship that isn't working as well as you would like it to, it's important to ask yourself what your role is in the dynamic and what you can change or do differently.

Here we look at how assuming responsibility for our key relationships can create extraordinary bonds with our self as well as with our partner, family, friends, and colleagues, and lastly, with the wider world around us.

Yourself. Think of your relationship with yourself. What voice do you use when you talk to yourself? Do you have a fierce and unrelenting inner critic that speaks to you in ways that are unkind, punishing, and unhelpful? Maybe every time you do anything 'wrong' it starts up. It could sound like a parental voice, a teacher, or a friend. Sometimes you might find it galvanizing. Maybe you think this voice helps you do better and strive for more. You might even tell yourself this: 'If I didn't have this voice to tell me I've done wrong and I must do better, I'd be nowhere in life!' But ask yourself if this is true. Is it really true that if you found a deep sense of self-compassion and love that you wouldn't achieve anything? Sometimes we have a deep need, a motivational need, to be perfect, and we use this as a stick to beat ourselves with rather like a poor working donkey being beaten up a steep mountainous path by an uncaring, cruel owner. This is probably not how you want to see yourself but if we endlessly strive for this unattainable status of perfection, we are that donkey and we will never let ourselves stop walking up that treacherous, exhausting path.

Letting go of the idea of perfection is vital, because there is no such thing. We are all flawed because we are human and our flaws – our fundamental vulnerability – is what makes us wonderful and attractive to others. The ability to love and care for our self, to name our needs, to let others into our life, gives us a deep sense of commitment to our self and all of humanity. This takes practice but if you let your interior guard down a bit and soften into a place of self-acceptance, whereby you speak words of support, care, pride, and joy to yourself, you will find your relationship with yourself changes in ways you previously thought would never be possible.

Partner. When it comes to our partners, it's helpful to think about our role in the relationship. What are your grievances and complaints about your partner? Now, think about how you can take responsibility and own your behaviour in the relationship. For example, I had a friend who was constantly complaining about her husband's indolence and how she had to do everything around the house. Over time I noticed that actually, although she was – and still is – a powerhouse of a woman, she was also not averse to martyring herself. She'd come home from a long day's work and then, in a rather passive-aggressive way, start cooking dinner, banging every pot and pan, and loudly chopping vegetables. She'd huff and puff as she dragged the bed linen off the beds to put in the washing machine. She'd noisily get the mower out and walk furiously up and down the garden doing the job she plainly thought her husband should be tackling. Meanwhile he would quite happily sit on the sofa watching sport and reading the newspaper. Many of us get locked into this behaviour and we fester away in anger and resentment. But what if we could find ways to communicate how we're feeling? In the case of my friend, why *would* her husband undertake those chores if *she* was doing it all? Sometimes we have to change our behaviour and we have to show the other person by our actions that we are going to change *what* we do and *how* we do it. Maybe your partner will change too, maybe not, and perhaps there are compromises to be made (if you can, pay someone to mow the lawn, buy a dessert that's ready-made, etc.) but focusing on the communication around these issues is what will change your relationship.

Family. In a way the members of our family know us better than anyone else, given they've known us all our lives. However, they may not know all the parts of us. Despite being adults, we can sometimes get very stuck in our childhood behaviours and positions in our families. At times, it's difficult for parents and siblings to see us as we are now rather than the child we were back then. For example, a shy child might have transformed into someone who has grown in confidence, who is good at managing their lives (maybe they previously couldn't manage that well by not having the voice to let people know what they needed), and who can speak up for themselves. A child who found it hard to tie their shoelaces or who had difficulties in social situations may now be competent and happy and act with great aplomb in all situations. Sometimes it's hard for parents to see their offspring as grown-ups – they may intervene when we don't want them to or treat us as if we're still eight years old. The way we can shift this is by taking responsibility for how we are when we are in relationships with our parents and siblings. If, for example, you have an over-protective mother, you can thank her for the love and care she has shown you over the years but then gently remind her of your age. Let her know you'd like to run your life in a way that suits you and you'd like her to respect that. Thanking family members for the care they have shown you – or pointing out the lack of care if that's how you are feeling – is a good way to broach your feelings with them. You can follow up your thanks by saying that you are now an adult who is capable of taking responsibility and that you'd like your family relationships to respect that.

Friends. Friendships are incredibly important to our lives, although it's useful to recognize that they change over time. If you think back to your birthdays in the past, who came to your celebrations? Some people may have been there every year since you were young, other friendships fade as new friends come and replace them. Most of us love our friends and enjoy their company. We celebrate and commiserate with them, we extol their virtues and downplay their 'bad' qualities. It's an oft-repeated statement that we don't choose our family, but we do choose our friends, and it's because of this that we can also choose to invest in them by taking responsibility for our part our relationships. One way of doing this is to commit to letting friends into our lives, allowing them to see *all* of us and not just parts of us. We might assume that if we let them see all parts of us they may no longer like us, but unless we can let people see us in our true form, our relationships will feel conditional rather than unconditional. We also need to accept that friendships change and sometimes we need to be able to let go of some of them. This isn't easy but if you become aware of the ones that aren't working for you – maybe you feel the other person takes from you without giving much back – you have options. You can let your friend know that's how you feel and that you have been wanting to raise this with them for quite some time, apologizing for not speaking to them about it previously. Then see if things change and, if not, make a commitment to yourself that you are prepared to let the friendship go.

Colleagues. Our relationships with our colleagues can take us into very difficult places in ourselves as these are generally not relationships that we have chosen. We choose our partners and friends. Our family is our family and they tend to choose us on a deep level because in a way we have no choice but to do the dance of the family and our blood and our lineage are entwined. Colleagues though are often brought into our lives in ways that are unchosen. Therefore, taking responsibility in these relationships can be very difficult. Although it's often true that we can create our work 'family' and we might have a work mother or father, or a work husband or wife, not all of us have this. Sometimess it's more tricky than this and at work, we'll likely often feel that someone is deliberately being difficult or trying to undermine us. We may think a colleague doesn't rate us or isn't a productive co-worker or a supportive boss. We can become very triggered and upset about what we *think* is true rather than what really could be true. It's helpful to understand that often we project our own fears onto others, as can be the case with imposter syndrome. If we feel we are not good enough for our job or our role and that, someday soon, everyone will find out, we will assume our co-workers will really see and know that we are useless. But this is something we are projecting onto them. It may well be that our co-workers think we are really brilliant at what we do. On the other side of this coin, our co-workers and bosses often have an assumption about what we may feel about them. This is where confusion lies. When you are thinking about any difficult work relationships, ask yourself: is your issue really that person or does that person remind you of someone else? Could it be that you could choose to see this person in a different light, a more positive one? Could you change the words, 'They make me feel useless' to 'I make myself feel useless,' and then choose to change those feelings? Remember relationships are a dance – if one person changes the steps, the other person also has to. They may not follow you into your dance – they may not know the steps and they may even leave the dance floor – but all of this heralds necessary change.

World. One of our major responsibilities is to really own how we are in the world. How do we treat our world and how do we treat ourselves in this world? Do we treat our environment with respect and compassion? Or do we feel like the universe is not behind us, that our life is hard, and everything is against us? If so, we can reposition this and see that we need to take responsibility for what is around us as well as how we treat everyone and everything in it. The universe will give us challenges and difficulties, but embrace these as opportunities for growth. This will allow you to raise your consciouness into a higher place and in higher service, committed to your own growth and that of the universe around us.

3 key points

1. Sometimes we have to be brave, stepping out of how we have perceived ourselves and others. We need a radical readjustment in order to see relationships as they really are, rather than through our own particular lens of hurt or pain.

2. We need to take responsibility for our part in the creation of the energy of a relationship, whether it is with a family member, partner, lover, friend, boss, or colleague.

3. We need to own up to our responsibility in a way that lets people access the more vulnerable parts of us. This then lets them respond in a way that can generate better and more fruitful relationships, rather than retreating back to defensiveness.

3 key tips

1. The Japanese art of kintsugi repairs broken objects, such as ceramics, using a lacquer made from or mixed with powdered gold. The repair does not aim to restore the object to its original form, but to a new kind of beauty – unique, original, and sometimes more beautiful than it was before. When you make the choice to take responsibility for your relationships, you are the source of that gold. It comes from within you. And even though you may not be fully able to repair a relationship that is irretrievably broken, you owe it to yourself to repair it in your own soul so that you are at peace with it.

2. Just because someone behaves in a way you find hurtful or difficult doesn't mean you have to act similarly. One way to consolidate relationships is to honour those who help you and look to repair relationships with those who might not be behaving in a way you would like them to. Consider extending generous gestures, taking action to repair with someone with whom you have a difficult relationship.

3. Hold people in your heart so that the broken relationships can be repaired in an energetic way. The other person may not be open to these gestures, but the connection will change for you to a happier, healthier place as you will have done your part in the act of trying to repair the relationship.

3 key actions

1. Take responsibility. This means you may even have to consider walking away from those who are not becoming conscious in the way you are.

2. Let others know why you are changing the way you show up in your relationships.

3. Show others what taking responsibility looks like – tell them, show them, help them.

Quiz
HOW RESPONSIBLE ARE YOU FOR YOUR RELATIONSHIPS?

1. You get home from work to find the to-list you left for your partner or family member hasn't been tackled. What do you do?

a) Sigh and feel deflated, you ask yourself why they've haven't done the tasks. Feeling incredibly let down, you set about getting on with the tasks yourself.

b) Feel shocked. Why on earth is the laundry still in the washing machine? Why has no one made any dinner? In the end, you turn in on yourself – it must be because no one cares about you. You slump down and feel exhausted and demotivated, which makes you feel even worse about yourself.

c) Get angry. What kind of lazy, uncaring person doesn't see how much help you need? Surely it's obvious what needs doing?

d) Remember you hadn't actually given your partner a list or ever really discussed or made a plan with your household about what needs doing. You realize that if you had been incredibly clear about your needs and asked people to meet them, in a way they could hear you, you would get more support than you do currently.

2. Your parents call to ask if you could give up some long standing weekend plans in order to take them to an event they really want to go to. What do you do?

a) You have two other siblings but on some level, you accept that it always falls to you to look after your parents. You tell yourself this will never change so you let your parents know you'll take them and you cancel your plans.

b) Feel completely conflicted. On the one hand, you honestly don't see why you should change your plans. Then again, you love your parents and want them to be happy. In the end, you decide not to do anything and see what might pan out even if it means you will be inconvenienced in one way or another.

c) Call up your siblings and lose your temper. You find yourself utterly enraged and call them both all the names under the sun then slam the phone down (and feel even more incensed when no one calls back and offers to take your parents).

d) You come to realize that in many ways you have set this dynamic up by being constantly available and dropping everything in order to help your parents. You also realize you have never voiced this to them or your siblings. You resolve to write a letter or phone them all up, or do whatever you need to do, to calmly let them know how you feel about this. In the meantime, you let your parents know you can't help them this time, but hopefully perhaps one of their other children could.

3. You have a friend who is constantly changing their plans and forever 'forgetting' the fact you've agreed to meet, so much so that it has really begun to upset you. This friend then rings to ask you to meet them for dinner. You know it won't happen so what do you do?

a) Say yes of course because you always do, and nothing will ever change.

b) Say yes but then feel really upset with yourself for not having called your friend out on the fact they don't stick to their arrangements with you.

c) You agree at first but then realize how upset you are, so you call your friend back and find yourself saying everything you've ever wanted to say, coming out in an angry and frustrated rant.

d) You calmly let your friend know that you won't be available for dinner but you thank them for inviting you. You then sit down and write out all of your feelings, exploring previous occasions you might have called your friend out before. Then you make a commitment to yourself to do things differently in the future.

4. At work, it becomes clear that a hugely important project with a looming deadline just isn't going to get done. The person in charge of the project asks everyone who is working on it to stay late until the project is complete. There is, however, special dispensation for those with children who are not asked to stay – you don't have children and this is not the first time the project manager has done this. What do you do?

a) Say yes.

b) Feel upset but agree to stay. You know how important the project is, although it rankles as it doesn't seem particularly fair that those with children get to go home.

c) Feel very prejudiced against, and you tell everyone this loudly. It seems completely unfair that those who don't have children are asked to work longer hours that those who do.

d) You tell the project manager you are going to have a think about this. It does seem to be a habit she is falling into by asking those without children to work longer hours than those who do, and you are wondering if there might well be a compromise position. It feels important to you that this subject is raised.

5. Your partner consistently buys water bottles made from single-use plastic. You are keen to reduce single-use plastic and are committed to living an environmentally conscious life. What do you do?

a) Just stay silent but recycle every bottle and hope it's not doing too much damage.

b) Feel frustrated and upset. You have raised this with your partner on many occasions but nothing is changing. Your only hope is that, over time and hopefully through effective public information campaigns, your partner will see the error of their ways.

c) Get incredibly angry when, yet again, your partner returns home swigging from another plastic bottle. You turn on them and explode about how selfish and thoughtless they are being and, in fact, this trait isn't just about the bottles – they're like this all the time in your relationship.

d) Get informed on the facts of what plastic does to the planet and then let your partner know. Tell them you feel strongly about this and their seeming lack of care about the future of the planet makes you feel very uneasy. You then request that they take your feelings – and the science behind the issue – more seriously.

RESULTS

Mostly As

You need to get empowered! Somewhere along the line you have probably dumbed down your needs and feelings because maybe you have felt they or you are unimportant. This means you find it hard to speak up and to be heard. It may even be that you feel you have no right to do this. You may also feel that you no longer know what your opinions and feelings are. Try checking in with yourself every day by asking yourself what you are feeling and then naming the feelings. The first step is to take responsibility for your relationship with yourself, then you can move on to trying out expressing your needs and feelings with other people.

Mostly Bs

You are on the way! You do know how you feel but you often find it difficult to truly let other people know how you feel about certain situations, along with what's okay and what isn't. It's important to tell yourself every day that you have a right to feel your feelings. If you turn your feelings in on yourself by not expressing them, they will start to affect how you feel about yourself. It's very tiring not expressing how you feel and this is where depression and exhaustion lie. Take a risk with people you know and try out asking for your needs to be met in ways that people can hear and respond to appropriately.

Mostly Cs

Your feelings come out in a huge angry rush. I imagine you find it hard to control your thoughts and feelings – it may even feel as if you are having a physical reaction to the perceived injustices done to you. This is why phrases such as 'a sudden rush to the head' exist. However, in order for people to hear you and respond to you, you need to take responsibility for your feelings. If you can practice the art of calmly explaining what you feel and why, people will respond to you in a more generous fashion. Try to create a self-soothing mantra that you can say to yourself every time you're about to explode, then imagine yourself letting others know how you feel calmly and with a deep sense of self-responsibility.

Mostly Ds

You are absolutely on the path to being accountable for your relationships – well done. You take responsibility for your feelings and experiences, and you are capable of letting others know how you view things and why. Keep on going. The more we can take responsibility and see how we project our feelings on to others, the better our relationships become. Name your feelings and needs, and practice the art of not being affected by other people's opinions of you.

Chapter 6

You have choices – make different choices

'Excellence is never an accident. It is always the result of high intention, sincere effort, and intelligent execution; it represents the wise choice of many alternatives – choice, not chance, determines your destiny.'

Aristotle

Once you've started taking responsibility for your relationships you can move forwards to the practice of recognizing that you have choices around what you do and say, and how you act. We all have choices about whether we listen, are empathic, change our narrative, and heal ourselves. Choice is a wonderful thing. When we come to realize that we do have choices, however small, we can start feeling a sense of agency in our lives. This means life isn't just happening to us, but we are actively choosing the life we want, with the people we choose to be with, in a way we wish to live. We often shut ourselves down to these choices, telling ourselves a certain path is too difficult or too challenging. Sometimes we find it hard to even become aware of the myriad options and possibilities available to us.

When we recognize we have the power to choose, it means we start focusing on what our choices are, allowing our brains to sift through them. Once our range of choices become clear, we can feel empowered to make them and galvanize ourselves into taking action. This might mean making changes in our work and home life to moving on from old relationships that are no longer serving us and being brave enough to seek out new ones. At the very centre of your capacity to choose is you – am I taking action to be a good friend to myself and to others? Or am I mired in inaction? Asking ourselves these questions is where having choices and being aware of them can fundamentally shift our relationships.

Making choices isn't always easy and I often hear this from clients in my therapy room. They struggle to make choices as so many options seem available for just about everything, from choice of flavoured yogurts to potential online dates. I acknowledge this struggle and I can reassure you that learning to make these choices is a skill that can be learned. Recognizing that we have the power to choose means we are taking active decisions rather than being stuck in procrastination. By taking the decision to make our choices visible to ourselves and then acting on them means we can *choose* to let people know we are not okay with the way they behave. We can *choose* to make better choices in order to improve our relationships. Furthermore, once we can connect with the true authentic intimate parts of ourselves – a sophisticated version of gut feeling – we can make our choices from a place of deep inner knowing.

In this chapter you will learn how to:

1. Find your choices by using your inner knowing, learn how to make these choices and then discover how they might change your relationships with others.

2. Reprogram your subconscious mind by practicing changing our thoughts and making different and better choices that will improve your relationship with yourself and those around you.

3. Embrace people who embrace you whilst being aware of what relationships aren't really working for you. Notice the people in your life – are you in a state of love, peace, joy, and gratitude with them?

Case study
STEPHEN

Stephen came to see me ostensibly because his marriage and life as a whole was in crisis. He and his husband Antony, who were now in their early thirties, met at university and had been together ever since – a timespan of over a decade. He said he loved his husband very much but that things had changed. In fact, *he* had changed. Over the course of a few sessions, Stephen told me his story. He was the eldest son in a very academically competitive family. His father stressed endlessly that Stephen must be successful so he'd been a 'good boy' (his words) and been accepted to the University of Cambridge. After gaining a first-class degree, Stephen got a job high up in the petrochemical industry. 'I earn a fortune,' he told me, and he'd bought a lovely Georgian mansion in the home counties of the UK, where he was busy redecorating and making a beautiful garden. Stephen and Antony were also hoping to have children.

It all sounded wonderful, a dream life for many people. Yet Stephen told me he was unhappy. He had come to realize he despised the industry he was working in. 'It's so competitive,' he said. 'I have to work long days and ultimately, I'm working for an industry that doesn't care about the world or the environment or anything really, and I've realized that I do. It's very important to me.' He told me his deepest wish was to sell the house, live in a more ecologically-responsible way, join environmental groups, turn vegan and, most importantly, give up his job. However, when he told Antony how unhappy he was and painted a picture of a potential future, he told him he found that hard. 'It's not who he married,' he said.

Once we'd worked together for a few months Stephen came to see that he was struggling because he'd never really been able to make choices for himself. 'I've always done what I was told – by everybody.' What Stephen was actually telling me was that he wanted change but that he didn't know how to even begin to go about it. His history of being told what to do by parents and teachers had left him unable to feel confident about the choices he faced in his life. If we have a family history of not being allowed to choose what we want to do, who we want to hang out with, who we want to date, or to select a career we want, our belief that we have the power to choose will be very weakened. We will not feel confident to make choices. We will potentially even minimize our own choices on the altar of taking responsibility for everyone else. For example, I have many clients who come and tell me they hate their work – they are not just bored but they are doing something that they actively don't want to do. When I offer the suggestion that maybe they change their lives and choose to do something they want to do, they look confused and scared. It's as if they have been told that it's not possible for them to feel empowered enough to follow their dreams. Somewhere along the line, their inner knowing has been questioned and possibly even quashed.

We all know people – and maybe it is us we know – that wanted to do X but were told by parents, teachers, grandparents, or friends that they should do Y instead. There may well be good reasons behind this, for example in the case of parents calling the shots, they tend to want their children to have a safe income, own a home, and be good citizens in steady jobs. This message may be conveyed by parents to a child in many different forms – conversations, feelings, fear of 'lack'. This means a child grows up with a sense that they can't follow their dreams but, instead, they must be a 'good' person and do what everyone else wants them to do. They may feel responsible for other people's happiness and that if they make different choices – the choices *they* want to make – they will be upsetting other people and letting them down. So, they keep on living a life they are not truly enjoying – ultimately, they are making compromises. This may all be fine for a time. In relationships and in life in general, we all have to compromise at times for the greater good and happiness of the majority. But when we hit a crisis we may well realize, in one form or another, that we are not doing what we want to do. We are not having the relationships we want to have and we feel stuck.

Change does not always come naturally to us. We are very used to being how we are in the world and functioning in the way we are used to functioning, and although that might not make us happy, it's what we know. However, in order to lead a contented and (for the most part) happy life where we feel connected to others and good in our skin, we need to make the choices that suit us. This will lead us to making better choices in our relationships and *that* leads to extraordinary relationships full of understanding and commitment. We need to embrace action as thinking can only take us so far – our thoughts won't change what we do unless it leads to actions.

HOW DO WE FIND OUR INNER CHOICE POINTS AND KNOWING

Learning what our choices are, along with assessing where and when to make them (our choice points) is a key step in improving our relationships. The main things we need to do is to practice listening to our inner voice. Your gut instinct – this is the part where your inner voice resides – will help you access your ability to make good choices. You likely have a sense of what this is – your instinct tells you when you suspect something isn't quite what it seems, it's the place where red flags reside. Ask yourself how often you have 'felt' something might be wrong but you didn't listen to your inner feeling.

It has been very well-reported that our gut feeling is real rather than something that might seem a bit far-fetched. Scientists now believe we have a second brain in our gut. The extensive network called the enteric nervous system that regulates our gut actually uses the same chemicals and cells as the brain both to help us digest and to alert the brain when something is amiss. There is copious medical research on this, not least by Dr Michael Mosley who has explored our gut's ability to communicate back and forth with our 'big brain' in his book *Clever Guts Diet*. According to research from Harvard Medical School[1], the brain and gut conduct 'crosstalk' so although the gut does not have the 'thinking' capacity of the brain, it does give the brain information about our wellbeing.

---

[1] See https://www.psychologytoday.com/us/blog/practical-wisdom/202101/the-gut-brain-connection and https://projects.iq.harvard.edu/hsci-report-2020/gut-brain-connection

We often ignore our gut instinct because part of us cannot believe that our inner knowing does actually know. Let's say you go for a job interview and somewhere along the line you realize this isn't really the job for you. Your gut instinct is telling you this – maybe the person who'd be your line manager is someone you are not responding well to, the job is not as it was described, the hours are too long, or the role is out of your skill set. Your true inner knowing is telling you not to take the job but you rationalize yourself away from your gut instinct. You tell yourself the job will be great, you need the money, you'll grow into it, and your would-be line manager might just have been having a bad day. This is how we talk ourselves out of listening to our gut instinct.

In order to make different, better and more empowered choices, we need to tune in to this instinct. It's the part of us that alerts us to danger, that feels uneasy, that tells us to alter our course of action. So, when we're making a choice and we have a 'feeling' about it, we need to listen and be curious about what that feeling is – ultimately, we need to be alert to this.

Tuning in to your instinct

Rather than ignoring your red flags, quietening down your inner knowing, and overriding what your gut is telling you, ask yourself what the feeling is. Here's an exercise to help you do just that. I practice naming the feelings in my body on a daily basis, as it's how I stay connected with my inner knowing. I first did this with Katherine Woodward Thomas as part of her 'self-love power practice,' which she writes about in her books *Calling In the One* and *Conscious Uncoupling*.

———

1. When a feeling comes up, such as a disappointment
or an upset, or you have a question you are asking
yourself, ask you inner self *what* the feeling is? It's not
an answer that comes from our thinking but from a
feeling that resides in the body. Close your eyes and
take some long deep breaths in and out. Breathe in
for a count of four and then out for a count of four.
Concentrate on your breathing and counting, and drop
your awareness down into your body. Then ask yourself
what you are feeling and let your gut respond.

2. Don't question what your inner knowing is saying –
just feel it and know it. It may be saying, 'This person
isn't for you' or, 'This job isn't good for you.' Just be
curious and connected to your body and the feelings
that are coming up.

3. Open your eyes and write down what your inner
knowing is saying.

4. Spend some time looking at what you have written.
How does it *feel* to you? Don't overthink it, just check
in with your body. Then think about what decisions
you can make around this. What possibilities and
opportunities might be available to you? What else
might be good for you? Try on how it would feel
to make a different decision and embrace a new
opportunity that might arise because of this decision.

5. Let your mind roam freely. Be creative and dynamic with this sense of new possibility and opportunity. Check in with how it feels to do this – really concentrate on this. The more we let new thoughts flood our body, the more we change our brain chemicals. Good feelings become our go-to state of mind rather than negativity and a sense of doom, along the lines of, 'Nothing can ever change.' Once we truly believe that this is not the case – and it isn't the case – a whole host of new possibilities and opportunities open up for us.

The problem with ignoring gut feelings

We often ignore our inner knowing. It's as if we can't trust ourselves to make good decisions and good choices. We often rationalize away what our inner voice is telling us, reassuring ourselves that, logically, this person is a good person, or this job will be brilliant. We talk ourselves out of listening to what we really need to know, and in doing so, we ignore other potential possibilities and opportunities. For example, if we long to be in a relationship, when we meet someone who could potentially be a partner, we might leap on that relationship before we've really had time to get to know this person and check in with ourselves about whether they feel right for us. We assume there will be no other possibilities or alternatives, but we need to recognize this is not necessarily the case. Being aware of our choices opens us up to truly getting in touch with our inner knowing and then daring to trust it.

EMBRACING INTUITION AND THE CHANGE IT BRINGS

If we are to make good and informed choices, we need to be attuned in a bodily sense, so ask yourself, what is your body telling you? We don't always have to act on it, but we do need to be aware of it and factor it in to making different choices. The more we practice this, the more listening to our inner knowing becomes a habit. And habits end up changing our brain chemicals, the more our brain gets used to doing it. The neurons in our brains are flexible (neuroplasticity) and the theory is that if we think good thoughts, we strengthen the parts of our brain that expects good things to happen. If we endlessly think negative thoughts, we end up strengthening the negative parts of our brain. So, if we make good and informed choices, our brain will become biased to that. It's the power of positive thinking that we want to embed. From there, we need to find the skills and capacity to let those around us know we want to change our relationship with them.

This isn't always simple. If our partner, friends, family, and co-workers are used to us behaving in a certain way, it's quite an adjustment when we start behaving in a different way. People may experience you as being difficult or certainly different. If, for example, we start calling people out on their behaviour towards us, when in the past we have been accepting, it might come as a surprise. There may well be a risk involved. The friend who is habitually late – which makes you feel as if you don't really matter to them – might well not like it when you point it out. Co-workers might not be okay at first when you start saying no rather than yes. Partners may find it difficult when you tell them what your needs are and how you'd like those needs to be met, especially if this is not something you have done in the past.

But once you change the dance, others have to change around you. If you stop doing a tango and start dancing a salsa, those around you inevitably have to adapt their dance steps too – their behaviour *has* to change. Some people might choose to dance off into the distance. They may not like the changes you are making, preferring it when you say 'yes' (even though you'd rather say 'no').

You may even find it a bit of a shock to see yourself as the 'you' you have never really known yourself to be – someone who is authentic, committed, communicative, connected with your deep inner knowing, and letting yourself be guided by it. This will help you to become available to connect to others in this deeper and more honest, open way. It might be difficult at first. But imagine how it will feel once you take ultimate responsibility for everything you do because your thoughts, words, actions, and deeds come from a place of deep inner knowing and intentionality. Everything around you will change, but you need to know how to change your relationships by letting people know about your different choices, in order to reach this seismic change. One way of doing this is to 'own' your part in your relationships and to be aware of your patterns, then you can let the people around you know about these new choices by engaging them in a 'change dialogue'. There is a version of this in Imago therapy called The Behaviour Change request.

How might a change dialogue go?

You can have a change dialogue with anyone – friend, family, partners, colleagues, and even with yourself. Sometimes we might need to change our relationships with people whereby we choose to take responsibility so that we're not just blaming the other person for everything. Let's take Stephen and Antony's situation as a useful place to explore how we might choose to change our relationships so that they can be closer, more rewarding, and with deeper understanding between ourselves and the other person. In Stephen's case, he needed to sit down and have a long conversation with Antony in which he took responsibility for the new choices he was making.

It could go something like this:

'Antony, I apologize for not taking responsibility for letting you know who I really am. This is partially because I didn't really know who I was. I can imagine it must be difficult for you to see me change and make different choices, and to see my values and morals change in such a determined way. I imagine you might feel confused and angry with me. You married a rich, ambitious businessman, not a vegan who wants to change the world and live in a yurt. I would really like us to have a dialogue about this so we can really hear each other.'

This way of relating to Antony is generous in spirit. By taking responsibility for the different choices he is making and offering to explain them to Antony – whilst also being willing to hear what he has to say on the subject – both Stephen and Antony can see how they can work together on these choices and what the outcome might be.

The key component for Stephen and Antony is that Stephen is taking responsibility for the different choices he is making – choices that are more authentic to him and reflect the 'real' him, rather than the him he thought he was supposed to be. However Antony reacts, he can know that Stephen is honouring their relationship by being honest with him. He is also creating firm boundaries, setting out what is truly important to him along with what is negotiable (where they might live, for example) and what isn't (his commitment to being vegan). The ability to make healthy boundaries is essential in all our relationships including the one with have with ourselves.

How to establish boundaries

In order to make different and better choices, we need to commit to making healthy boundaries. These tend to be around modes of behaviour, like how we speak to and treat each other, how we can put people's needs at the centre of our life (such as with a partner) and asking them to do that for our needs in return. The place where boundaries reside is one of respect, kindness, and authenticity. However, as we explored in the previous chapter, many people don't actually know what boundaries are, especially if they were not consistently present in childhood. If you had family members who respected your boundaries one day by knocking on your door before entering your bedroom (as you'd requested) but, the next day, just walked in regardless, it might well be very difficult for you to locate your boundaries.

Here's a checklist I often ask my clients to keep in mind when establish boundaries:

1. Healthy boundaries feel important and necessary to you but are not overly controlling.

2. They tend to be based around behaviours that are appropriate and/or inappropriate.

3. They allow you to have your needs met whilst asking other people to respect your feelings and wishes.

4. They're located in your value system so there can be a moral basis to them.

5. They're not used to force other people to bend to your wishes but are appropriate to you.

6. They help create relationships that feel safe because everyone knows where they stand.

7. They create respect – we respect someone else's boundaries.

8. If our boundaries are constantly crossed and disrespected it gives us helpful information about that relationship.

FROM PROCRASTINATION TO ACTION

One of the most positive consequences of taking responsibility for our actions is that it helps reduce our tendency towards procrastination. If we can master the art of truly tuning in to our deeper knowing, we can access what the 'right' thing to do is. It may not feel obvious at first. We may feel we don't really know what the right thing to do is but once we start really pausing, breathing, going into our body, and asking ourselves with great and respectful curiosity what our gut is telling us, we will start to access our inner knowledge. The more we do this, the more confident we will become at tuning into it. We will then become more confident in the choices we make.

This position of not knowing what to do can feel uncomfortable but, for many, whilst they say they hate procrastinating, they can't seem to get out of the habit. This is because we need to find the capacity and skills to make new habits, and we need to consistently practice them. Research has shown that it takes 90 days for new habits to form[2] and for the brain to rewire and code this new behaviour into our system. It's one of the reasons this model of making a new habit by not drinking for 90 days is used widely in addiction programs such as Alcoholics Anonymous. We need to take action by practicing our new habit of making good choices, opening ourselves up to new possibilities, choosing to surround ourselves with good people who love us, and choosing to be decisive and dynamic even if procrastination has been our go-to way to behave.

---

[2] This research is very complicated, but you can read more here https://deborahbyrnepsychologyservices.com/creating-new-habits-using-the-21-90-day-rule/#:~:text=We%20can%20use%20the%2021%2F90%20day%20rule%20to,longer%20to%20make%20a%20habit%20a%20permanent%20one.

In many cases, procrastination is a form of defence. If we don't really make any decisions because we are vacillating between one choice or another, we can never really be blamed if what we decide to do or feel turns out to be the 'wrong' choice. However, there is immense joy in finding the ability to harness the power of knowing our choice points and then acting in a direct and energized way. Imagine moving forwards in your life in a dynamic way rather than being mired in the misery of procrastination. Once you can truly take ownership of your good, healthy choices, the outcome of making these choices is relatively immaterial because you know you have made the best choice for you. This is the difference between dynamic people and procrastinators – those who can make choices easily have a confidence in them and they don't sweat the small stuff.

You might wonder about making wrong decisions but if you commit to learning from your decisions, you can never really make bad choices. Job disappointments, heartbreak, financial loss – all of these and many more life events are extremely painful, and we can spend months (even years) beating ourselves up for making poor choices. However, when we learn from these decisions and, most importantly, where we make the decision from, we start making better choices and open up new, exciting possibilities. If we make choices from a panicked and anxious place, our brains become so clouded we often make poor decisions and choose the wrong things. When we pause and breathe, and notice what our gut is telling us, we can weigh everything up and make good decisions. Our brain then codes this into our subconscious and we turn from procrastination towards action.

The power of pause

All change starts with thoughts and feelings, and then action. Your brain is very sophisticated – and it is very good at sifting and learning new things, sorting stuff out, and putting things in categories. It helps analyse and keep things – whatever those things might be – regulated. Think of it like watching a baby pick up a new toy – they roll objects of different shapes around in their hands, feeling textures, temperatures, and sensations, and the information is all fed back to their brains. Your adult brain still does the same thing – when you have feelings and thoughts, your brain sifts them like a sorting office whereby envelopes get put in different but appropriate places. Once you have identified your thoughts and feelings around your choices, you need to take a pause. This gives the brain the opportunity to work out the best way to act.

So often in life we are quick to react – we get defensive, shout, cry, freeze, or run away. But if we give our brains the chance to do its work, breathe steadily, and connect with our inner knowing, the actions that stem from this place will be calm and considered rather than rushed and panicked.

Once you identify your thoughts and feelings, you can take action from an empowered place to make different and better choices. If you need to make a choice about something, before you rush to action list all of the possible actions you could take. Then sit and look at them. Try identifying an action that feels congruent and affective, and perhaps not the action you would usually take. Let your brain do a bit of sifting. Challenge yourself to do things differently from now on and notice the effect this has on your relationships.

HOW TO UPLEVEL YOUR RELATIONSHIPS

With yourself. We can choose to have a better relationships with ourselves. Instead of letting our negative thoughts take over, we can make the decision to prioritize positive ones. We can choose to grow the skill of not letting our punishing critical voice take precedent over the part of ourselves that loves and cares about us deeply. The more we can connect with an inner, kinder voice, the more we will feel empowered to make different and better choices when it comes to our feelings about ourselves. Notice all your thoughts for an hour (if an hour seems too long, try five minutes). See how many negative ones you have; really notice them. There will probably be many more than you thought there would be. Try to turn all those negative thoughts into positive ones. The more you practice this, the easier it will become to think more positively and then to make choices from a positive and empowered place.

With your partner. We can make different choices about how we react to our partner. If we can take responsibility for the actions we take, we can choose to react differently. This helps bring a new intimacy into our relationships as we dare to show our vulnerabilities and become honest with our partner about our needs, whilst also being open to hearing about theirs. This requires the ability to have the dialogue whereby you open up, telling your partner about your innermost, deepest feelings whilst taking ownership of them. You are daring to be authentic and honest with all the wonders that brings. It might well feel difficult at first but by making the choice to share openly and with deep honesty, the possibilities for your relationship will flourish.

With your family. Family relationships are difficult to shift because our habits and patterns with our family are so ingrained. Families tend to come in 'systems'[3]. This term comes from the practice of systemic therapy, which looks at how family dynamics work. These 'systems' are very difficult to break. However, just because your family does something 'this' way or 'that' way doesn't mean you have to do it the same way for the rest of time. Change can be a good thing, bringing new, more empowered relationships as we start to bring a fresh approach to the patterns in our family. It can be a game changer for one person to make a different choice in how they want to be within their family. Perhaps you have labels in your family (the 'clever' one, the 'funny' one, the 'black sheep,' etc.) and you don't like the label you have been given. By highlighting your desire to choose to step away from these labels you can shift your whole family dynamic to a healthier place.

With your friends. If we choose to take different actions and choices with friends, we can create a new level of closeness and enjoyment. It's key to ask and be aware of who you are surrounded by. Are you choosing relationships that are positive for you? Or are you in relationships with people who feel like a negative influence? Make choices to be around those who love and care about you and are 'radiators' rather than 'drains,' that is, they're warm-hearted and generous-spirited and they fill you with good feelings when you see them. They are genuinely interested in you and vice versa. Drains take all your energy by complaining and putting themselves and others down – consider distancing yourself from these friends.

---

[3] https://www.aft.org.uk/page/whatisfamilytherapy

With your colleagues. Work can be a very difficult place to make different choices. We often feel stuck in a rut at work. But know you have the capacity to be more open with your colleagues, including your boss, about how you feel. Make the choice to let people into your world a little more so that they can get some idea of what's going on for you, and they can then react accordingly. Once you change what you do and make the choice to be congruent (whereby you are exactly what other people see), you will always know you are reacting from a place that has boundaries and sits well with you. What confuses people is if they feel someone is not really being themselves (that they are being incongruent) – this feels unsafe and unsettling.

With your world. The way we choose to treat our planet and those that inhabit it, from the tiniest creature to the largest one, is important. It takes a sense of responsibility to do this differently. Try out one new habit, however small, that helps embrace our planet rather than destroy it. It's amazing how one person's small change of action can ripple out – every journey starts with one step, however tiny and apparently insignificant.

3 key points

1. It takes one person to shift a relationship and that person is you. Once you make different choices, others have to react to this. It's like changing a dance – if someone is doing the tango and another person is salsa-ing away, someone has to shift.

2. Our ability to make different choices comes from our wise adult centre. It's a part of ourselves that we need to learn to access by getting in touch with our inner knowing, taking responsibility by naming our choices to ourselves and others, and then setting healthy boundaries.

3. All choice is about action. So, choose to identify your possible actions then do them differently. Once our new choices and actions become embedded in our brain, they will start to feel natural, becoming our go-to way to react.

3 key tips

1. Pause. This is a concept much embraced and used in Buddhism and it's a brilliant one for everyone. Before you do anything else, pause, then question the patterns of how you respond. For example, if you are a person who is quick to anger and someone says something that makes you feel angry, before you fly off the handle, just pause. Then breathe. Then respond.

2. Check in with yourself and ask if your reaction is helping build good relationships or hindering them. Remember, it take 90 days for a new habit to be formed, so be alert and attentive to your reactions, and monitor your feelings by checking in with your inner knowing.

3. Take responsibility for your actions and choices. As long as you can let others know you are choosing to take responsibility for your part in your relationships and actions, change is ultimately possible.

3 key actions

1. Make new choices and then act on them, which means making a conscious decision to do things differently.

2. This means actually *doing* things differently – present your needs, react in a different way, get out of your old story, and act in a new way towards others.

3. Let people know why you are doing this – take responsibility but always let people know what's going on. Action means showing up in a different way and taking responsibility for the outcome, and if you need to let some people go, so be it.

Quiz
HOW ATTUNED ARE YOU TO MAKING DIFFERENT CHOICES?

1. You have been single for many years and you're very keen on finding a partner. You have signed up to many dating apps and been on quite a few dates that haven't really gone anywhere. The other evening you met a person you liked, however a couple of things they said slightly jarred with you, such as the slightly disparaging way they spoke about other people, including their ex. They want to meet up again. What do you do?

a) Tell them no immediately. Although you liked them and thought you had a good time you are wary of who this person might be underneath. You just will not countenance anymore heartbreak, disappointment, and failed relationships.

b) You say yes immediately. This person was funny, good looking, replies to texts, and ticks all the boxes on your list. Okay, some red flags might be gently fluttering in the breeze but you really want to meet someone so you leap at the next date offer.

c) You sit down and breathe and then let your brain sift through your feelings. You ask yourself various questions. Once you have some sense of the possibilities and opportunities ahead of you, knowing there will always be other opportunities ahead of you, you write down all your options so you can have a sense of the best way forwards.

d) Say yes – nothing ventured, nothing gained – but remind yourself to stay super-attentive to this person's words and actions, and vow not to get involved in a relationships too quickly.

2. Your office is holding a team-building weekend at a hotel. It looks fun – lots of activities and bonding exercises – but you have social anxiety and you usually hate these types of things. What do you do?

a) Send an email to your HR team making up an excuse about why you can't go but then feel terrible. You know you'll be missing out and you'd like to bond more closely with your colleagues, but you just can't face it.

b) You say yes but then immediately regret it and chastise yourself for not finding a reason not to go. You are terrified your anxiety will kick in and you won't be able to cope, meaning everyone will judge you.

c) You sit and have a think, weighing up the pros and cons of going. You let yourself work through your fears. You also let yourself imagine actually being there with your colleagues and enjoying your time together. You let that positivity flood through you and then ask yourself what's more true – that you'd have a terrible time or that you'd actually enjoy it? You make your response from this thoughtful, embodied place.

d) You say yes and then spend some time making carefully considered escape plans just in case.

3. You love your family and you spend a lot of time with them, however over the years you have come to find their lack of care for the environment very difficult to say silent about. They don't recycle anything, saying it's a waste of time. They don't use their food compost bin and they leave the lights on all night. What do you do?

a) You sit on it. You find it difficult not to say anything but you are very worried that if you raise your issues everyone will turn on you and get angry and upset.

b) You decide to say something but find yourself blurting everything out and getting very upset and tearful. Your family don't receive it well, which is exactly what you feared.

c) You write down what it is you want to say to your family, also taking your time to own your responsibility for not bringing your concerns up earlier. You then list all the possibilities of how everyone might do things differently going forwards, making these steps easy (for example, refilling water bottles rather than endlessly buying new), so that your family might sign up to attempting to change some habits.

d) You make a plan and get very over-excited listing things like compost bins, water filters for the tap, non-plastic water bottles, glass bottles for milk, etc. You can't wait to tell your family exactly how we can all save the environment, feeling sure they will get swept along by your enthusiasm.

4. Your partner, with whom you are generally happy, has a few irritating habits. For years you haven't let them know about how irksome you sometimes find some of their behaviour. One, in particular, that bothers you is the fact that they don't stack the dishwasher 'properly.' At first you were okay with it but now it has really started to bother you and you have come to the inevitable conclusion that they wilfully mess up the cutlery draw in order to annoy you. What do you do?

a) Try to say something but end up not saying anything as you feel guilty for making a fuss and you assume that if you have any form of confrontation your partner will leave you.

b) Get so frustrated at their lackadaisical attitude towards spoon stacking that one night, after a long and exhausting day, you lose your temper. You start shouting at them and then burst in to tears when you see the confused look in their face.

c) Really try to work out what it is about your partner's behaviour that is bothering you and why you haven't brought it up before. You find a way of sharing this with your partner, which hopefully will open up a more thoughtful dialogue between you whereby you can both be heard – you know this will help you find a way forwards.

d) Realize you need to change how you act so, rather than dumbing down your needs, you think it's important to finally tell your partner how you feel but you are not exactly sure how to do this.

5. You have a friend you've known since childhood and there has been this assumption that you are close. You don't see each other that much and over the last couple of years you have realized the two of you have changed and you don't have so much in common any more. You also find it distressing that when you do meet, all your friend talks about is how down they are and how terrible their life is. Nothing you do seems to change this and you are struggling with it as it leaves you feeling frustrated and sad yourself. What do you do?

a) Try to bring it up, despite not feeling sure why their behaviour is distressing you. You tell yourself that this person has been your friend forever. How could you turn your back on them now?

b) You finally get cross with your friend and find yourself telling them one day that you are sick to death of their moaning and complaining and that you no longer want to be their friend. Then you feel terrible – sometimes you just don't understand why you behave this way.

c) You sit with your feelings, becoming curious about why you feel this way about this person and taking responsibility for why you end up feeling so low when you leave them. You let yourself really feel into this friendship, asking yourself if there may be ways you can help and support this friendship if possible.

d) You try to come up with a way of letting your friend know you find it hard to see them when they are low. Invariably though, you get stuck telling them at length about the good things in their life and why they should be more grateful, and wouldn't it be great if they cheered up a bit?

RESULTS

Mostly As

It's possible that you find yourself thinking in 'black and white'. Outcomes are either A or B. You fear that if you raise your concerns or upsets with other people, they will turn on you, judge you, or leave you. This inner assumption often leaves you disempowered as you do (sort of) know deep down that you just might be able to voice your needs, wants, and feelings. However as you struggle to know how to do this you probably fall back on doing nothing. Try going into your body every day to ask it what it's feeling and what it needs (go back to page 113 for a reminder). Listen deeply to the answer and just let it flood through your body. If you practice this soon, you will find yourself becoming stronger both in your knowing and listening to the calls for action.

Mostly Bs

You want action! But sometimes you are not sure how to go about it and at times everything seems out of control. Close friends have shared with you that they find your anger difficult but you have always told people, 'This is how I'm made.' But ask yourself this – do you like being this way? Anger is an energy and, like any other energy, it has a driving force behind it that can be very useful at times. A lot of action is born out of anger because it's an active rather than a passive energy. However, you need to utilize it wisely rather than shooting from the hip because you find it hard to control, meaning it's quick to fire up. Practice the breathing exercises before you take action; know that your heart is in the right place and build from there.

Mostly Cs

Well done. You have obviously spent a lot of time and energy on making different choices and reacting from a different place from where you did in the past. You have probably asked yourself the question, 'What choices can I make inside of this emotional centre that mean I can shift relationships?' The key part of this is to drop down into your centre before you make decisions. You are able to pause before you react and also to check in with your inner knowing so that you come to situations with a sense of new purpose. Keep on going but also be very aware of the new choices and possibilities opening up around you. Sometimes we need to make a different choice to the ones we have made before because this is how new agreements are made.

Mostly Ds

You are getting there. You have got the basis of how to make different choices but you are not quite there yet. Sometimes you get so exuberant at the idea of changing things that you go a bit over the top. Your emotions often get the better of you so you might rush at things rather than pausing to take a bit of time to think about what you are feeling and what actions you might take. Use the pause. Your heart is in the right place, now connect with that energy and then check in with your inner knowing to act from that place – this wise adult – rather than the wilful, excitable child. It's not that this wonderful child part of you shouldn't be honoured – it probably makes you quick, quixotic, and changeable, and people may well love this about you. However, when we make choices, it's important to make them from a place of wisdom rather than frothy excitability.

Chapter 7

Be rigorous about where you put your energies

'He who lives in harmony with himself lives in harmony with the universe.'

Marcus Aurelius

What tows us towards a future whereby we have extraordinary relationships? The simple answer is, love. The more expansive explanation is love, commitment, belief, trust, and advanced communication skills. Simple as it is, though, love is the most complete answer, because we can bask in the knowledge that love is an unlimited resource. We can love in abundance. We have the capacity to make choices to extend love and empathy towards pretty much anyone and everyone we meet. This is a choice, and the only way to have extraordinary relationships is to commit to this. Commit to being the sort of person who can generate love and kindness. Commit to being in the world as someone who has extraordinary relationships with people. This chapter is going to be slightly different. This is because it is the pinnacle of the journey we have been on. We have followed our 'hero's' journey. We have learned many skills and now is the time that we expand this knowledge even further outwards beyond ourselves and others, and out in to the universe. We are taking actions from this place – this place of knowledge and belief.

Sense into it. When you are with people, ask yourself, 'Where do I feel the energy in my body?' Our gut instincts are a pretty good indicator of friend or foe, as we looked at in the last chapter. So, it's imperative that we are rigorous about where we put our energies and that we have a sense of what our future relationships can look like and feel like. Whilst I honestly believe we can transform pretty much *any* relationship – once we shift, other people have to shift – we can also choose who we want to be in a relationship with. We may decide to hone our relationships down to the significant ones, but we can also show up in life as an abundant and kind human being who smiles at pretty much everyone. We can put all our senses into embodying love.

The more we can invest in creating and maintaining extraordinary relationships, the more this sense of wellbeing and happiness reflects outwards. Imagine it expanding across the universe almost as if our shift in our mindset and behaviour has caused an earthquake under the water that spreads out and positively affects the lives of all those around us. This will lead others changing their relationships too, so this sense of connection and wellbeing floods outwards creating positive, seismic change.

This is where we have been heading. The themes we have covered in this book build on this knowledge of how to change our relationships. This is our goal – to feel the effect of transformation and to make heartfelt commitments to ourselves, to our families, partners, friends, colleagues and, ultimately, the universe.

In this chapter you will learn how to:

1. Work out who you are in this world. Do you walk through the world as a person who is downcast and negative, whilst dimming your light? Or are you emanating love, warmth, and wellbeing? How might you change from one to the other?

2. To harness the power of really knowing what your relationships are about and where they are centred. The key to having extraordinary relationships with everyone including yourself is to become supremely adaptable. It is important to hold your centre, to keep strong, firm, and committed in your sense of self, but it is equally important to be able to adapt to other people.

3. Focus on your relationship with the universe. What are your beliefs about it? Do you have any beliefs at all? How might a sense of yourself being surrounded by a greater power help you?

Case study
MAUDE

Maude came to see me after her adult daughter had died. 'She was alive one minute and dead the next,' Maude told me. She had been on holiday at the time and had missed calls from her daughter letting her know she wasn't feeling well. By the time Maude had finally received them, her daughter had died. There seemed to be no reason for her death and the autopsy didn't reveal any particular cause. 'It's inexplicable,' Maude kept repeating to me. It was her mantra. Maude was herself 87 years old. Her daughter had not yet turned 60. One reason why Maude couldn't get through her grief was the unfairness of it all. She felt that, at her age, there was little point in trying to understand anything. For her, life had become unliveable. She became depressed and told me she just wanted to die.

Of course, what has happened was terrible, and I told her this. It was important to acknowledge her deep pain, sadness, and confusion. But also whatever happens and no matter our age, there is always a glimmer of light even if it's tiny. I asked Maude if she could accept this, that there was a tiny piece of light somewhere in her heart, in her soul. I offered that, if we choose to invest in this light, it will get stronger – the flames will burn more brightly and maybe the darkness in our souls might lift a bit. I pointed out that she had grandchildren and great-grandchildren, along with friends and wider family. These relationships were there for her, to help her, and for her to help them too.

Over the weeks Maude began to brighten a bit. It wasn't easy. Grief resides in us as an unwelcome guest. But I let Maude know that if she let it take up a large permanent residence in her head she might never feel happy again – even if for a few seconds. And no one can live a life of pure misery 100 per cent of the time. She started to go out more and she began to see friends. She took up painting, which was a hobby she used to enjoy in the past. She found a local class and began to have coffee afterwards with people from the class. She resumed going to church and reinvested in her own personal relationship with a higher power. She connected with her family and found a friend who would drive her over to see her grandchildren. Gradually the light began to shine a bit more brightly.

What do we do when life throws us curveballs such as this? How do we reconcile ourselves with tragedies that seem unfair and unprecedented? And what has this got to do with our relationships to others? It seems sometimes as if what we are being asked to deal with is too much for us to handle. We're exhausted. We can't cope. Maybe no one around us understands us, or at least that's the story we are telling ourselves (and it feels convincing). Maybe we've had a crisis of faith.

Yet we need to find a well of something else deep inside ourselves. We need to see that glimmer of light, invest in it, and try to get the flame to turn up a bit every day. We need to fully let ourselves know that we can do this, that even in our darkest times this tiny, warm flame exists.

Part of this is about belief – the belief that we can have better relationships, work on being a better person, strive to listen, respond, make different choices, and change our narrative. But the key thing is to take action. Once we have put structures in place, we need to make sure that we act from this place – it's the active participation in these processes that will engender change.

In the end, what Maude offered up to me about what had made a difference to her – what had pulled her out of the mire of depression – was repositioning how she felt about her daughter's death. She would always be sad, it would always be a terrible loss. But it had woken her up to the fact that, whatever age, it was important to put our energies into relationships. It meant she could slightly shift her narrative from one of feeling intense sadness, regret, and depression, and turn towards one of hope. What had her daughter's death taught her? Many, many things and one was that she could still have a relationship with her grandchildren (and their children), and their love for their grandmother wasn't based solely on the fact she was their mother's mother or grandmother. She realized the love they had for her was for *her* – for her as a person who was significant to them. The bond was strong and active, and Maude took great solace in this. It meant she had to readjust her narrative around these relationships and invest in a future whereby she put her energies in to these vital loving bonds.

It is connection that carries us forwards and our belief in whether we can connect with other people or not. The love of her children, grandchildren, and great-grandchildren meant a lot to Maude. By closeting herself away, she was sinking into a black hole. She wasn't telling anyone (bar me) how or what she felt. She was containing her grief in a tightly lidded urn and it was swirling around in her, unbeknownst to others. In the end, it was destroying her and keeping her away from the connection with others that she most desperately needed. Inside of her something changed. She made a choice to do things differently, to invest in her capacity to form good and healthy bonds with other people and take the risk of sharing her feelings, in order to be helped and supported.

WHY DO SOME PEOPLE 'SURVIVE' WHILST OTHERS DON'T?

In Maude's case, relying on existing relationships, as well as forging new ones, helped her cope with her grief – ultimately, they helped her survive it. In chapter three, we looked at how some people who have had terrible things happen to them manage to flourish whilst others don't. Some individuals who suffered adverse childhood experiences (ACEs), such as being chronically emotionally undernourished or even abused, go on to have successful, steady lives. Others who, on the face of it, haven't had such dramatic things happen to them, seem mired in pain, procrastination, depression, and apathy.

So, why do some survive? There might be many answers to this question. Often people who have suffered from ACE build up a certain level of resilience – it's that sense of, 'Well, if no one else is going to do this for me, I'll jolly well have to do it for myself.' As a society we place much value on the ability to be resilient. However, if we become over-resilient, we might pay the price by not being able to form open-hearted relationships with others. There is a lot of emphasis put on the quality of being resilient and it's often promoted as the number one important quality we need, especially in children, to survive life. However there needs to be a balance that is struck between the healthy quality of being resilient and people who then become over-resilient. (By that I mean those who are so capable and apparently in control that no one feels able to approach them or offer them help for the fear of being rebuffed.) This over-resilience leaves us isolated and potentially exhausted, rather than competently managing our life, our emotions, and our relationships.

It's vitally important that we can put our energies into having a great relationship with our self. No one can ever truly support and love us more than we can support and love our self. Often, we can mask our inability to truly connect with our self by overly connecting with others. We may recognize this feeling within us to look after other people before we look after ourselves. We help others survive and flourish whilst not in any way putting that care and level of energy into our own wellbeing, so we need to find the skills to take care of our self.

Looking after yourself

Relocating where we put our energies, so we can have the help and support we need, enables us to have wonderful relationships with our self and others. Keep in mind the upcoming points to invest in your wellbeing:

Take the risk of sharing your feelings. Often people think that no one will be interested in them or be available to help them – but this is not true. There are good-hearted people all around us, but they can't hear, help, or connect with us if we are closed off. We need to take the risk of being vulnerable. Knowing what we need and asking for it is one of the best capacities to grow within our self.

Be curious. Think about what feeling like a burden might mean to you and where it has come from. Are you a burden to yourself? We need to cultivate lightness of being, to see things for what they are. Some things are serious, some are not. We can differentiate between these states of being by investing in better connections between ourselves and others. Practice reaching out and talking to someone, anyone.

Let yourself fully feel your feelings. Sometimes we fear our feelings might overwhelm us and that, if we fully let them out of the bottle, we will never get them back inside. Even more, we fear we will not survive them and instead be permanently overwhelmed by them. However, we are feeling beings and, once we're in touch with all of our feelings – the good and the not so good – we have the power to control them, which means we can choose how we feel rather than being a slave to them.

Visioning: connection

In order to connect with your feelings and a sense of energetic support and love, try this powerful tool whereby we connect with our bodies and link our mind-body experience.

Find a safe and relaxing space, close your eyes, and imagine yourself connecting with everyone you love, as if you are the centre of an atom or the hub of an energy field. You are a humming source of energy – feel the vibrations running through you. You are full of love, warmth, and vibrant energy. Then imagine all the people you love and care about standing around you – really see them. They are smiling at you and you are smiling back at them. You are filled with a wonderful sense of love, warmth, kindness, good will, and benevolence. Let these feelings flood your body. Then imagine you are bonded to all these people through a silken string connecting you together in a light, tender way. The string comes from you and shoots out, connecting to all these amazing people around you. Your love pulsates through this connection – really feel into this. See all the people you care about in an even more vibrant way. Love them and then send even more love to them. Imagine all the people behind them whom they love and see the silken strings reaching out to these people too, and send even more love and good will. Now everyone else is also sending love and the energy force around you is growing stronger, wider, and bigger. Continue this process until you have sent love, goodwill, and kindness to everyone in the world – to people, animals, and your environment. You are one big ball of fiery, energetic love, and all the love is also coming back to you. Take it all in. Bathe in it. And let yourself truly know how wonderful it is to feel this way. Your feelings are on fire and you feel warm with wonderful love and a generous energy of spirit.

Know that this is accessible to you at any time. It's from this place that you can walk through the world as someone with a huge heart making wonderful connections. Lean into what it looks and feels like to be someone who is connected to everyone and everything. What does it feel like to have this knowing, this faith, that whatever happens, you can choose to react differently, to become a person you didn't even know you were? Someone who has the capacity to create extraordinary relationships. Take this deep inner knowing and position it within you so that it becomes your way of being. This is how you are. The more you embody this, the more natural it will seem to you.

Surviving Trauma

People who survive trauma have something in common. They can adapt their relationship with themselves – that is they do not sink into victimisation – and they take actions both internally and externally, which means they are rigorous and vigorous about where they put their energies. By this I mean that they have come to some realization that, although the trauma may well reside within themselves, it does not define who they are. This means they have an adapted relationship with themselves. They realize they were this type of a person before the trauma and now they are a different type of person, and they're able to adjust how they viewed themselves, how they view others and how they view the world from this new place. They do not let the trauma become 'the thing'. If we do let trauma become 'the thing', it takes over our very selves and we cease to really recognize ourselves, what we need or what our feelings are, and we can get very stuck in this place of depression and anxiety – we view the world through that lens. We view other people through that lens. We even view ourselves through that lens.

Those who can make that room a part of themselves and live with it and almost grow from it, use the trauma to inform them about major and important things in their life: how they've lived that life before, the sorts of relationships they had, their view of how life is.

Those who survive trauma, then somehow bravely use it as a tool for growth are connected and attuned to their own wants and needs, which then makes them connected and attuned to those of other people's. They are able to source themselves from themselves – they take personal responsibility – but they may also have a great faith in the power of something bigger, whether that's their community or a higher power. For many people having a sense that they are joined to something on a more divine level brings great joy, peace, and happiness. It gives some form and texture to their life and existence. For many people it gives them a purpose, and having a purpose is vital when we are considering actually how to live our life. So instead of bumbling along not really taking any form of responsibility for our autonomy and expecting other people to run our lives for us, we actually feel we are put on the planet to do something significant even if it is very, very tiny. If you are not spiritual, become in tune with your world and your environment in a way that feels nourishing but also expansive and peaceful – everything is in its rightful place. The energy is one of abundance and it exists all around us.

BE RIGOROUS ABOUT WHO YOU SURROUND YOURSELF WITH

A secret of successful people is that they are very aware of who they have around them. That's not to say successful people only hang out with other successful people, but those who are alert to where they put their energies have realized there is little point in rescuing people and expending all their wonderful energy especially when, often, little change occurs. Many of us have had the experience of trying to help someone, spending hours listening to them, giving them advice and generally looking after them, only to find that nothing changes. There is little point in trying to rescue someone who doesn't want to be rescued. So part of this is also growing the capacity to work out who to invest in, in terms of your energies, your learning, your expanded vision, and ability to have extraordinary relationships. And, of course, those not to invest in because all of this will basically fall on deaf ears or will land like seeds on fallow ground. A person may *say* they want your help but it's actions that lead to change, not words. So be careful to be rigorous of where you put your energies and have some sense of what these future relationships – and any relationships you have now that are going to change because of the work you have done through this book and the learning you have achieved – will look like. Those future relationships will look and feel very different from the relationships you have with people now, even if it's with the same people. This means you can then reflect this outwards and across the universe as you grow and learn. It's very important that we model good and inspiring behaviour and, once we start doing that, we will notice that those around us do this too.

So, it is important to be aware of all of our relationships, given we are the sum of the people we spend time with.

The key is to be able to recognize our relationships for what they are. Think of your friends and ask yourself, 'How do I feel when I leave this person? Am I filled up or depleted?' Apply this question to everyone you know – your partner, family, friends, and colleagues. What this means is that you have information about people. You know whether you should invest in them or not. You can make decisions about where you put your energies and that's really important to know. You can also let people know, 'actually, I'm not sure this relationship is working for me, so consequently I think I'm going to put my energy elsewhere.' Or 'I'm going to back off a bit,' or maybe, even more radically, the two of you could actually come up with a way of healing your relationship so that you are both trying, you are both putting energy into it, and you are both working towards a common future of realignment.

Make an active decision to put your energies into being more positive. Not everyone will like this, because it's like putting up a mirror to other people. When you make an active decision to get happy, to invest in yourself, to create healthy relationships, to turn negatives into positives, not everyone will like it. In previous chapters, we've explored why some people around us are silently invested in us *not* changing. Be rigorous in noticing which people around you are 'for' you and those that are not. For example, quite often people get stuck in their bonding over their wounds – their misery and depression cloaks them and starts to attach to them like a second skin. It's as if this is who they are and they don't want to risk shedding this skin. These people attract other people who also feel the same way they do. Like attracts like. Then the wounds become the 'thing,' so much so that this becomes all anyone ever talks about and experiences. Notice if you have any relationships like this. If so, try to gently extricate yourself from these even if you are faced with resistance from others.

Sometimes we have to be prepared not to be liked. We cannot be liked by everyone and we need to settle this within ourselves – not everyone is our friend. Not everyone wants the best for us even if they say they do, so be alert to this. We are cultivating the rigorous ability to have extraordinary relationships but that doesn't necessarily mean that everyone will like us. Sometimes seeing someone thrive is not easy and some feel a temptation to want to rain on another person's parade. These are not your people, they are not your tribe and you do not want them around you if possible.

Practice the rule of thirds with the people you surround yourself with: one-third of those around you whom you love, trust, and deeply care for; one-third for people you can help and mentor; one-third for those from whom you can learn, such as mentors, authors, and podcasters (or whomever you find interesting and inspiring)[1].

How to find out what's important

It's essential to ask yourself where you are in the list of who and what you find important. In my therapy room, I often

---

[1] This is a concept that has served me extraordinarily well, and one I first heard from Jon and Missy Butcher in their Lifebook programme, available on the learning platform Mindvalley.

ask clients to list who and what is important in their lives –
invariably, their list begins with their partner, children, wider
family, pets, and homes. Sometimes they are far down the list
below pretty much everyone and everything (and sometimes
they're not even on the list!). If this is the case for you,
concentrate on putting yourself at the top of your list. You
need to be at the centre of your life. It's not selfish, it's selfless.
If you are not functioning at your full capacity, it will be
difficult to engage in the energy it takes to have extraordinary
relationships. Here are ways to fill your cup:

Reach out. If you really admire someone and want to know
more about them, take a risk and contact them to ask if they
could mentor you, give you some advice, or offer up five
minutes of their time to connect with you. Be clear about what
you'd like to engage with them about. It's amazing how many
people want to offer their time to other people especially if it
is clear what's needed from them.

Learn. Engage in learning – sign up for webinars, be active and
present in them, get curious, and ask questions.

Engage. Work out your needs and interests in your life along
with what might stretch you. Maybe you want to practice
transcendental meditation, take a degree in a new subject, or
learn a language. Keep your body and mind active, focused,
and engaged.

Volunteer. This is a great way to connect with like-minded
people whilst also doing some good in the world. What do you
care passionately about? From the welfare of older people,
helping refugees in your area, or supporting your local library,

there are always a wealth of opportunities when it comes to volunteering.

Socialize. Make time for family and friends. Be very clear with yourself about who you like to spend time with and then actively spend time with them. Think of the activities you like to do together: cooking, going for walks, hanging out, listening to music, going to a gig, enjoying Sunday lunch, etc.

Make time for yourself. This is of prime importance. Really check in with yourself on a daily basis about what you need, then choose to put energy into that, whatever it is. Whether it's 10 minutes to meditate or go for a walk, a quick nap, seeing friends, having a swim, or going to an art gallery. Be very aware of what it is you need in order to function in the best way possible. We might not be able to meet all of our needs all of the time but, at the very least, we can help ourselves by tuning in to what they actually are.

A SENSE OF PURPOSE

It's vital to have an idea of where we are heading in life. Rather than just bumbling our way through directionless and being led and influenced by others, we need to have an idea of how we want to live. What might you like to be doing with your time? Where might you want to live? Who do you want around you? It's also important to have a sense of what future relationships might look and feel like.

In order to do this, we need to know how to harness our own sense of self. Part of this requires us to monitor how we react to people. For example, do we get bogged down in their problems, so much so that we become overly empathic and people-pleasing? This is where we need to be able to shift into a different state of being. It's from the place of knowing that we can adapt to other people – our centre is strong and so, instead of losing our inner sense of self and 'leaking' into other people, we can stay true to ourselves whilst empathizing with others. There is an immense power in being adaptable but this doesn't mean having blurred boundaries and an indistinct sense of self. It means knowing who we are, what we want, and how we can show up with others as someone who can be aware of their needs. We can be empathic towards others, honest, and build mutually supportive and beneficial relationships. The ability to shift our centre – that is, to be able to mutate into different versions of ourselves – is what makes us adaptable. It helps us hone in on our internal antennae so that we can mould ourselves into a state of being that helps everyone become the best version of themselves that they can possibly be. This is where real change lies.

In order to do this, we can practice visioning our sense of the future. If you can create this sense of your future in your body, every day you will be more attuned to the resonance of it. It becomes not just a belief but a realizable future. If you take five minutes a day to visualize what it would be like to live in this future – where you are having wonderful relationships, you're emanating warmth, openness, adaptability, and the willingness to create connection – you will start embodying that in your daily life.

___

Visioning: future relationships

To vision effectively just find a safe and relaxing space. Close your eyes and take a deep breath.

Feel into your sense of purpose – where you are going and what you want in your life. What is your purpose? Let yourself fully know where you are heading and, once you have this in your mind and body, let yourself know you can live your life from the future backwards. You are now this person with amazing relationships and you can walk through the world as someone who is already living this life. Sense it, feel into it. Have a sense of what this future relationship with yourself feels like and be very curious to all the sensations you might be feeling. Do you feel warm? Is there a bubbly sensation within you? Connect with every part of your body.

Make a commitment to endeavour, every day, to bring some light and happiness into another person's life and see how that makes you feel. Imagine yourself walking through the world as if you are already this person with these relationships. Which ones do you invest in and which ones do you have to say goodbye to? Really feel into this and see what comes up. You may feel sad to let some people go but your inner knowing will tell you which ones sustain you and which ones do not.

___

HOW KNOWING WHERE TO INVEST YOUR ENERGIES CHANGES YOUR RELATIONSHIPS

Action is where change lies and so knowing where to invest your energies means you are deciding to move towards a life in which all your relationships are positive and engaging. Be mindful of how being rigorous in where we invest our energies can benefit our relationships.

It firms up and supports your sense of self. Once you can connect with the part of you that is future-oriented you can really get an embodied feeling of yourself in an authentic manner – your true self becomes a reality and you can embrace the world from this place.

You can offer this sense of self to your partner or a friend. How might they benefit from being with someone who is available to meet them in a new way – with warmth, love, tenderness, and understanding. In many ways you are modelling to others how you want to be treated and inevitably your partner or friend will start to respond differently.

You can start to build your apothecary of emotions. This means letting yourself feel your feelings and then imagining yourself taking these emotions from your body (using an imagery such as a wand), placing them in a bottle, and labelling it – do this for all emotions: happy, sad, listless, joyous, etc. Know that you are beginning to build up an entire pharmacy of emotions – see them in your mind's eye in their bottles stacking up on your shelves. All emotions are there, from pulsating love to a sense of quietude and inner peace. This means that whatever you are feeling and whatever comes up with family, friends, work, etc. you have the capacity to take a break from difficult feelings and reach for a different jar. Once we know we have the power to change our feelings, to respond differently, to draw on different and myriad resources, we can find the energy to invest in our relationships.

Friendships are, in many ways, more complicated than family relationships. We often feel we can't walk away from friendships, and we often extend a tolerance towards our friends that we don't give to our family or partner. But not all friends will be good for us. It's important to invest our energies wisely and carefully so that we have enough emotional reserves to invest in them, rather than giving out all our energies to all and sundry.

Remember extraordinary relationships take work. They don't just happen but emerge and grow because we make a commitment to them, we nurture and commit to finding learning even through rough patches. This is where true relationships lie, in the realm of the difficult. Relationships are easy when all is going well, but it's the tough times when they're tested, as with a colleague or friend you might struggle with. Dig deep, find compassion, engage, re-energize, tell yourself what's more true about this relationship, and then move it into a calmer future space.

Belief. The ability to have a sense of this, to feel into what our relationships could look and feel like, is a key to transformation. When we can find a body sensation of how we might feel to have these extraordinary relationships, we will find that it is increasingly possible for these relationships to happen. This lies in the realms of belief and faith. Can you trust your ability to be rigorous about where you put your energies? Can you commit to growing your relationships? Can you let yourself know what this might look and feel like? We are responsible for our relationships, not other people. The more you can recognize good relationships, the more of them you will have.

Be very aware to look for signs. Once you start looking for signs that the universe is on your side, that it is a benevolent place and that is has your best interests at heart, you will see evidence all around you. You are just thinking of someone and, seemingly out of nowhere, they call you. You are wondering what to do when something crops up then and there that helps you make a decision. You wanted to buy the apartment of your dreams and it fell through only for it to come back to you six months later. Be very aware of what is happening around you. When you start opening up your awareness and curiosity to all the signs around you, you will be amazed what changes. It's as if you are opening up a new expansive energy within yourself, one that is genuinely delighting in all that life has to offer, whereby everything is a learning experience even if it hurts. Growth hurts. It's as if you are emerging from the birth canal into a new reborn life and way of being. All your relationships have to change as you are changing. You can make the wise and active decisions as to how that change might look and feel. It is you who is in charge of your own destiny when it comes to having extraordinary relationships.

3 key points

1. Imagine living your life from the future backwards, as if you are already living the life you so desire and you are having the relationships you want. Feel into this and know that every day you are the person you have always wanted to be, having the relationships you truly desire.

2. Walk through the world as someone who is emanating love, happiness, and kindness. Make an effort to connect with people. It's amazing how positively people respond when you engage with them, even if it's only for a minute. Notice people: give someone a compliment; smile at passers-by; engage in a conversation; laugh with people. Notice how others light up around you and how that light also lights up in you. Let yourself be nourished by this as you endeavour to nourish others.

3. Be very aware of your feelings and remember you can access your apothecary of emotions at any time, helping you master your emotions whilst giving you the ability to choose different ones. This will help transform your relationships as you break out of your old patterns and choose to behave differently towards other people and yourself. The curiosity you possess about your interior emotional life will inform your everyday being.

1. Make a decision to radiate *more* – more love, more care, more goodness, and more positivity – and see how the relationships around you shift and change. Remember one-third of your relationships is for those you love, one-third is for helping others, and one-third should be upwards-looking, towards mentors and teachers (in whatever form they might take).

2. Put yourself in the centre of your life. It's only when you do this, when you learn how to invest in yourself and put your energies there, that you can truly have extraordinary relationships. You need to be powered up like a battery in order to bring intention and action into your life.

3. Look for signs. Where are you in your own world? What relationship do you have with the universe? Treat our universe with deep respect, acknowledging everything has the right to be here and honouring that. Be kind to pretty much everything (even wasps!), knowing that everything has its place here in our world. Once you start giving to the universe, you will find it gives back in abundance. Trust the deeper knowing of this.

3 key actions

1. Wake up every day and check in with how you intend your day to go – stick with that intention.

2. Actively take responsibility for actions and deeds.

3. Invest in some form of belief, however that might be and in whatever form.

Quiz
HOW FAR DOWN THE LINE ARE YOU WITH CREATING EXTRAORDINARY RELATIONSHIPS?

1. Your next-door neighbour has noisy parties every weekend then chucks all their bottles out without recycling them. This is beginning to get to you. What do you do?

a) Nothing. You don't know how to go about raising the problem or what to say. You worry your neighbour will get angry with you and you just want peaceful relationships.

b) You totally lose it. You bang on the walls. You then get all their bottles out of their bin bags and smash them on the ground in front of their door. You've had enough!

c) You self-righteously make a BIG DEAL of very obviously recycling your own bottles. As you do, you yawn conspicuously when your neighbour is looking, complaining loudly of not getting any sleep and saying that maybe if the noise continues you might have to let the council know.

d) You tolerate it for a while then, one day during the week when you know the neighbours probably won't be tired and hungover, you knock on the door and ask if they're available to discuss a problem. You let them know you have no problem with them having parties

but you'd like to talk about reducing noise levels after
11 p.m. You also let them know you'd like to help show
them how simple it is to recycle bottles, explaining the
day of the week the recycling truck comes.

2. You are let go very suddenly and inexplicably from a job
you loved and thought you were good at. There seems to be
no rhyme or reason for this and no explanation given. You are
just asked to clear your desk and you are frog-marched out of
the office. How do you deal with this?

a) You go into a deep depression. It all seems unfair.
You get stuck in grief and you shut down and withdraw.

b) You get angry and rail at the universe. You weep and
wail. You cannot sleep. You feel utterly overwhelmed.
You cannot stop crying and that makes you even more
angry.

c) You go into a state of shock. You want to reach
out and talk to others but you can't seem to find the
capacity to do this. You feel ashamed, assuming you
must have done something wrong.

d) You grieve your job. But you also find enough
energy to find some counselling. You are able to be
curious about what you need. You check in every day
with what you need and you attempt to give this to
yourself. You ask other people to help and support
you. You try to learn something from this situation
on a daily basis.

3. You and your partner have split up and the divorce is finally through. It's been a long and painful process, you have a lot of regrets and also anger towards yourself and your ex. As you go to collect your decree absolute a rainbow suddenly appears right in front of you. How do you react?

a) You shut yourself down to any thoughts about this. How can it be possible that the sight of a rainbow could mean anything? You have no belief in this type of sign or interpretation of signs and think it's a sop to the masses. You'd rather stay mired in your misery than trust this small ray of light.

b) Why is this happening now? The appearance of this makes you sad and angry. It's no help when it comes to easing your pain. Where was the rainbow when you were married?

c) You feel gladdened by seeing it. You don't have belief in anything particularly spiritual but if you did, this would really help you know there's potentially a bright future ahead.

d) You let yourself take it all in. You are attuned to signs and seeing this gives you some reassurance. You let yourself really take it in and then let yourself know that this is the benign universe's way of letting you know it will all be okay.

4. A group of close friends are going on holiday to Ibiza. They have asked you to come but your partner has requested you don't go as, timewise, it affects the holiday the two of you were planning and it will also mean a hit on your finances. How do you respond?

a) You let your friends know you can't possibly go and then you spend hours on end telling them how sad and depressed you are about it, making sure your partner is in ear shot.

b) You get really cross with your partner. How dare they force you to choose? You get so angry you end up walking out and you fall out with your friends too – how dare they not understand the position you are in?

c) You feel so conflicted. You suffer from FOMO so the idea of your friends all having a good time without you really affects you. Then again, you do understand your partner's concerns.

d) You drop down into your body and ask yourself what's really going on. Then you take the decision to share this back with your partner. You are honest about your feelings, letting them know you'd really love to go away with your friends. Maybe there could be a compromise?

5. Your sister, who you love and are close to, reveals to you one night that she is having an affair with a married man who works in her office. His wife gave birth two months ago and yet he is telling your sister he will leave his wife. She asks for your advice. What do you do?

a) You are stunned into silence. You cannot recognize your sister as someone who would be in love with a man like this. You don't know what to say, so you say nothing at all but then hate yourself for not having responded and you feel confused.

b) You completely lose your temper. What on earth is your sister thinking of? You know she has always been very judgmental of women that have affairs with married men, especially if they have children, and now she's doing it herself.

c) You let her know that whilst you understand offices can breed many affairs – and she's not the first woman to have had an affair with a married man – you feel rather confused, disappointed, and upset, especially about the information around the small child.

d) Your initial reaction is to be pretty taken aback, but then you realize your sister is asking you for help and therefore it's important for you to find some words and feelings that are helpful for her. You are aware they may not have to be your feelings but you ask yourself what is it that your sister needs from you right now. You then try to answer from a place within you that is helpful, rather than judgemental.

RESULTS

<u>Mostly As</u>

It might be very helpful to think about your energy levels. It may well be that you feel lacking in energy and have a tendency to look on the downside, meaning it's hard to get enthusiastic about anything. Maybe you find yourself feeling quite depressed at times. The result of this will be that often you don't actually tell people what your needs or expectations are. Without this people might find it hard to connect with you as you seem closed off at times. Your fear may be that while you do *feel* emotions, you find it really hard to let people into your world. By not expressing your needs, your sense of future relationships might feel doomed as you assume nothing will change. But remember things do change but the change has to start with you. We often talk about how to 'manage' emotions – that is, how to bring our energy levels down and manage extreme emotions and modes of behaviour. What we don't really talk about is how to power ourselves up. The fear may be that you will be overwhelmed by your emotions, but trust the fact that you can contain yourself very well and imagine powering yourself up like a battery-charged lamp.

<u>Mostly Bs</u>

Whoah, slow down! You have the opposite problem to answering mostly As. Sometimes you need to take a deep breath and have a pause. Energy is your friend but sometimes it can become overwhelming and you lose your temper. It might feel really difficult to stay in control at times. You might feel as if you have steam coming out of your ears. However, conserving your energy is important. Once you have learned that skill you can then decide where to expend this energy and on whom. If people find you overwhelming, it will be hard for them to make genuine heartfelt connections with you. You might find you struggle with deciding who your real friends are and some people might find you a bit intimidating. Try feeling into the future relationships you so desire and get a sensation of them in your body. Calmly breathe this into yourself so that you have a real experience of what it might be like to have calm, kind, and nurturing relationships. Do this every day – the more you do so, the more you will be able to recognize these relationships when they exist. It also to help your current relationships become less reactive and more calm and consistent.

Mostly Cs

You're nearly there. You're investing in and building the capacity to be aware of where you're putting your energies and what these relationships could potentially look like in the future. You are able to recognize your own wants and needs, and have no doubt grown this capacity to meet other people's wants and needs. You might wobble in this sometimes though, because it's not easy to change the habits we have formed over a lifetime and commit to doing things differently. Keep on going. Read back over the chapters in this book and think about embodying this work. The more you feel attuned to these new relationships the better they will be, and the more easily you will recognize them. You will also be able to sort the wheat from the chaff and let the relationships that are not working for you go with grace and kindness.

Mostly Ds

Well done! You are doing a great job at being rigorous about where you put your energies and then having a sense of what these relationships might look like. I imagine you have spent a serious amount of time embodying this work, visioning how these relationships feel, and what they entail. This is important work – the more you can walk through the world investing in these relationships, the more joy you will feel in your life. This, in turn, means you are bringing joy to other people's lives and this has real meaning. If you can let these feelings emanate out of you like a pebble dropping into the water and out across the universe, you will create lasting change for yourself and others.

End note

All change starts with hope and my hope is that you, the readers of this book, take away practical tips on how to have extraordinary relationships with absolutely everybody. I hope that there have been some 'ah-ha' moments whereby you have either recognized yourself in this book, or perhaps realized there are a few simple things you can do that will bring greater happiness and contentment into your life and the lives of those around you.

Books are not written to be read just once – they can be delved into as and when. There is much to take on board in this book (the subject of each chapter could be a book in itself!), so I would encourage you to re-read each section or those that particularly resonate with you. Use this book as a guide to help you through your relationships in life and with life itself.

All journeys start with one step, however small or insignificant that step might feel to you. But remember this: even one tiny, infinitesimal change leads to bigger change, so your next step is to make a commitment to doing things differently.

It might look like taking responsibility for your actions or choosing to show up at work differently. It might be making a commitment to meditate every morning or doing a body scan (see page 113) to check out how you are feeling on a daily basis.

The wonderful thing about life is that you are living it and, if you have read this book, I am making a grand assumption that you are curious, you are conscious, you are committed.

If you'd like to take this work further, turn to page 252 for other books and websites that will help inspire more learning and exploration. Learning appears just when you need it to so relax, enjoy, practice your new-found skills, and watch your relationships blossom.

I am standing right there with you.

In love and faith and wonder.

If you want to know more, and find out more on how to have extraordinary relationships, you can go to:

lucycavendishextraordinaryrelationships.com

Glossary

Abundant relationships:
Relationships (relations with and to others) that are flourishing and fruitful.

Attunement:
Aware of and in harmony with some principle, ideal, or state of affairs; sensitive to someone's needs, desire, values, etc.

Authenticity:
The quality of being authentic and genuine; the feeling of being truly one's self.

Boundaries:
Something that indicates bounds or limits; a limiting or bounding line.

Childhood wounds:
Emotional scars that are left from traumatic experiences or negative relationships with parents or caregivers during childhood. These wounds can manifest in various ways such as fear, anger, and isolation, and can continue to affect us in our adult lives.

Imposter syndrome:
A psychological circumstance in which sufferers doubt their potential, and experience a repeated terror of being revealed as imposters. No matter the evidence to the contrary, those experiencing imposter syndrome will not believe they deserve good outcomes for themselves.

Inner knowing:

A capacity to lean into the universe's power as a guide, deducing information without it being explicitly revealed. Also known as higher self, intuition, innate knowledge or sixth sense.

Source fractures:

The psychological or psychiatric consequence of a traumatic event; impairments, disorders, mental harm, suffering, damage, or dysfunction caused to a person as a direct result of some action or failure to act by some individual.

—

Acknowledgements

No book gets written from a void and this one is no different. It has been formed from the theories, ideas, experiences, and connections that I have been honoured to have with and from my coaches, mentors, friends, and partners, along with my children, family, and life. The learning in this book lies on the foundation they all offered up to me.

I am standing on the shoulders of generous giants. These people and their teachings need deep acknowledgement and gratitude from me – and *they* themselves have all paid deep respect to things they learned from.

To be more specific, I learned the active listening technique in chapter one during my Imago couples' training. I learned it from the wonderful Dr Sophie Slade but the Imago founders and authors of many books, including *Getting the Love You Want*, are Dr Harville Hendrix and Dr Helen LaKelly Hunt. I first heard of how to utilize empathy in my counselling training at the Mary Ward Centre in London from Cecilia Jarvis, and this is all based in Carl Rogers, the founder of humanistic psychology.

The blanket work and shifting energy exercises were something I first experienced in the high-ceilinged former schoolroom in the magical Hambleden Valley with Andrew Wallas, the Modern Day Wizard and business alchemist.

My biggest gratitude is to Katherine Woodward Thomas, bestselling author of *Calling In the One* (CITO) and *Conscious Uncoupling* (CU). Many of her teachings inspire many practices in this book and I learned them in my CITO and CU training. All of Katherine's practices are referenced in the book. If you are interested in furthering the practices in this book, this is a wonderful way to start and on page 249, I have listed sources. Also, great respect and love goes to the community Katherine has created – all coaches and participants. It has changed my life.

My learning was also expanded by the content available on Mindvalley, the online and in-person inspirational learning community, and its Lifebook programme, with teachers Jon and Missy Butcher.

All gratitude to Sarah Thickett, my editor at Quadrille, Tamsin English for copyediting and Alice Hill in Publicity for all their hard work – this book would not exist without the holy triumverate.

The point I feel important to stress is that the learning goes on. For some people it may start with this book. For others it builds on life experiences you already know. What this book offers is a chance to think and do things differently. You will all make your own meanings of this – some aspects will resonate deeply, some not as much, which is how teaching and learning works. So, take what works for you and in turn you send that out – by hanging your relationships so they are extraordinary, others will follow your lead and change *their* relationships, and on it goes.

This is how change happens.

'We are what we repeatedly do. Excellence, then, is not an act, but a habit.'

Aristotle

References

Katherine Woodward Thomas, *Calling in the One: 7 weeks to attract the love of your life* (Harmony/Roedale, rev. ed 2021)

Katherine Woodward Thomas, *Conscious Uncoupling: 5 steps to living happily even after* (Yellow Kite, 2015)
(www.katherinewoodwardthomas.com)

Anna and Andrew Wallas, *Call Off the Search: The Modern Wizard* (Cadogan, 2013)

Andrew Wallas, *Intention: How to tap into the most underrated power in the universe* (Aster, 2019)
(www.andrewwallas.org)

Dr Joe Dispenza, *Becoming Supernatural: How common people are doing the uncommon* (Hay House, 2019)
(www.drjoedispenza.com)

Harville Hendrix and Helen LaKelly Hunt, *Getting the Love You Want* (Simon and Schuster UK, reissue edition, 2020)
(www.harvilleandhelen.com and www.imagorelationships.org)

Mindvalley (www.mindvalley.com including Lifebook with Jon and Missy Butcher)

Further reading

Marcus Aurelius, *Meditations* (Penguin Classics, 2006)

Eric Berne, *Games People Play: The Psychology of Human Relationships* (Penguin, 2010)

Brené Brown, *Daring Greatly: How the Courage to Be Vulnerable Transforms the Way We Live, Love, Parent and Lead* (Penguin, 2013)

Dale Carneige, *How to Win Friends and Influence People* (Vermilion, 2006)

E. H. Erikson, *Childhood and Society* (Vintage, 1995)

Sue Gerhardt, *Why Love Matters: How Affection Shapes a Baby's Brain* (Routledge, second edition, 2014)

Neville Goddard, *The Power of Awareness* (Tarcher, reprint edition, 2013)

Stephen Grosz, *The Examined Life: How We Lose and Find Ourselves* by (Chatto & Windus, 2013)

Edith Hall, *Aristotle's Way: How Ancient Wisdom Can Change your Life* (Bodley Head, 2018)

Thomas A. Harris, *I'm OK, You're OK: A Practical Approach to Human Psychology* (Arrow, 2012)

Dr Amir Levine and Rachel S. F. Heller, *Attached: Are You Anxious, Avoidant or Secure? How the Science of Adult Attachment Can Help You Find – and Keep – Love* (Bluebird, 2019)

James F. Masterson, *Search for the Real Self: Unmasking the Personality Disorder of Our Age* (Free Press, 1990)

Alice Miller, *The Drama of Being a Child: The Search For the True Self* (Vintage, 2008)

Michael Mosley, *The Clever Guts Diet: How To Revolutionize Your Body From The Inside Out* (Short Books, 2017)

Susie Orbach, *In Therapy: The Unfolding Story* (Wellcome Collection, 2017)

Esther Perel, *Mating in Captivity, Unlocking Erotic Intelligence* (Hodder & Stoughton, 2007)

Philippa Perry, *The Book You Want Everyone You Love to Read* (Cornerstone Press, 2023)

Dorothy Rowe, *The Successful Self: Freeing Our Hidden Inner Strengths* (HarperCollins, 1993)

M. Scott Peck, *The Road Less Travelled* (Arrow, reissued edition, 1990)

Polly Young-Eisendrath, *Love Between Equals: Relationship as a Spiritual Path* (Shambhala Publications, 2019)

Managing Director Sarah Lavelle
Commissioning Editor Sarah Thickett
Copy Editor Tamsin English
Proofreader Emma Bastow
Design Manager Katherine Case
Head of Production Stephen Lang
Production Controller Gary Hayes

Published in 2024 by Quadrille,
an imprint of Hardie Grant Publishing

Quadrille
52–54 Southwark Street
London SE1 1UN
quadrille.com

The content of this book is the opinion of the author and is not intended as a substitute for professional medical advice, diagnosis or treatment. Always seek the advice of a qualified health provider with any questions you may have regarding a medical condition. To preserve client confidentiality, names, events and identifying characteristics have been changed.

Cataloguing in Publication Data: a catalogue record for this book is available from the British Library.

text © Lucy Cavendish 2024
design © Quadrille 2024

ISBN 978 1 83783 113 5

Printed in Spain